Knickers for Aunt Alice

Mike Stenson

MIKE

P.151 mıGHt Inl¡ Bo

YOUR RETIREmenT.

Mke Plun

Knickers for Aunt Alice
First published in Wales on behalf of the author
by
Bridge Books
61 Park Avenue
Wrexham, LL12 7AW

A CIP entry for this book is available from the British Library

ISBN 978-1-84494-054-4

Disclaimer
Please be assured that no actual living thing was harmed in any way, nor persons, alive or
deceased, purposely offended or even indicated in the course of writing this book.
All events are construed from my own imagination and observations.

Printed and bound by
Cromwell Press Ltd
Trowbridge

Contents

Foreword

Knickers for Aunt Alice is a compilation of observations, occurrences, conversations and thoughts, self observed, overheard or imagined, that have been put into verse, containing varying degrees of exaggeration, accuracy, honesty and imagination to encourage a chuckle, a situation of self-recognition or one of total disbelief!

> Do I do that? I don't do that!
> Do I say that? I wouldn't say that!
> Am I like that? I know someone who is!
> That's impossible! Isn't it?

They cover situations of past and present, joy and sorrow, bizarre and chaotic, the sensitive and ludicrous. All are included, the young, the old, the tame, the wild, the parent, the child, the past, the present and the fictional. If you like it, read on and enjoy it. Laugh aloud or be emotional, doubt it or believe it, but above all – imagine it!

With gratitude to ...

... my wife, Barbara, who came to appreciate that, 'I'm going to scribble for a few minutes', was rarely just that and who encouraged me to publish them in the first place.

... all of those who read the completed scribblings for me, enjoyed them, and also encouraged me to publish them.

... the lady who set my scribblings to type in an acceptable book form, often after numerous corrections.

... Thomas for capturing the 'poetic characters' from the verses to create the cover queue.

... all of the publishers who declined my request for publication – 'we rarely publish poetry', 'we are booked solid for two years', 'there is no profit for us in poetry' – you aggravated a streak of self-determination I always knew to be there.

And finally, to all who will take it up and read my *Knickers for Aunt Alice*, smile, imagine and enjoy it.

A Full Day of Shame

The room is alarmed by the look on your face,
Body language, total electric,
No one dare say a word out of place,
That look, quite apoplectic.

It seems someone, has half-inched your wheels,
Sole means of your transportation,
Not a word have you uttered about those who steal,
That look, suffice indication.

Glowing with fury to the top of your head,
A vessel will surely burst,
Words not forthcoming but your message was read,
A tongue-lashing or even worse.

Slowly, so slowly, you eased back from the boil,
Temper in steady decline,
Body unwinding like a spring in a coil,
Calmness returning with time.

Words spat out soaking all with the spray,
Your message requiring no voice,
Wheels had gone missing sometime in the day,
Leaving walking the only choice.

Load bearers had gone, the rest had remained,
Left locked and without a mark,
Your transport was left where you could reclaim,
Why yours where others were parked?

You'd secured your transport with its own lock of steel,
Beyond mere casual attention,
Everyone now knew how this theft made you feel,
But thought you might give it a mention.

The strong language you used took all by surprise,
No words were even repeated,
We'd all thought of you as quiet but nice,
Foul temper never intimated.

As you cooled down and your awareness returned,
The events began to emerge,
You'd parked your transport up tight to a fence,
By a lamp-post, close to the verge.

Not being able to unlock the chain
Your wheels were lifted for spite,
Leaving behind bars, saddle and frame,
All that remained of your bike!

Once mirth had subsided all were agreed,
Finding wheels, the only aim,
Our time was yours, true friends in your need,
All in the room felt the same.

We returned to the spot where those wheels had been,
Searching the smallest space,
Questioning strangers about what they had seen,
Then came a familiar face.

The car came to a stop, blues flashing on top,
Your wheels on view in the boot,
The felon inside handcuffed to a cop,
A bloke in a filthy suit.

Then your eye caught the face of the nicked one,
Something stirred way deep in your brain,
Recognition arrived with no place to run,
Your dad, now a full day of shame!

A Lesson of Life

I met a lady in a mobile chair,
With darker roots than her tinted hair,
Full of life and so few cares,
Chomping on a bacon butty.

It seemed most things would set her off,
Start her laughing, so much, she'd cough,
With butty debris covering most of us,
A lady without self pity.

That chair, each day, her transportation,
Lacking lower body movement, not motivation,
To all that she met, pure inspiration,
A true lesson in the meaning of life.

Tucked in snug, hiding silent limbs,
A fate undeserving, no matter the sin,
This ladys heart showed all where to begin,
Use what you have and just do it!

No movement at all through feet or legs,
But a vibrant brain in a forgiving head,
A lady for leading, not one to be led,
Determined to live every day.

The cruelty of life she'd met head on,
Tackled it, beaten it, then moved on,
What sadness it brought, now long since gone,
Each moment, so precious, she knew it.

She talked, she smiled, she laughed out loud,
No matter just one, no matter a crowd,
Immobile and sitting, but tall and proud,
Her past suffering, forgotten, forgiven.

Each one that she touched, she left them a mark,
Bacon butty, a smile, a piece of her heart,
Her life wasn't over, just made a new start,
No movement didn't mean, no living.

No matter how defeated, how far down we may go,
That lady had given us, something to know,
Each life is a one off, no matter the blow,
Use every moment, enjoy it!

Ablutions

There are those who like to shower
And those who prefer a bath.
There are those who soak for hours
And those who do it for a laugh.

There are those who submerge in bubbles
And those who enjoy ice cold.
There are those too young for troubles
And those with the aches of old.

There are those who are just relaxing
And those who have to dash.
There are those who throw in the washing
And those who scrub the cat.

There are those who snack three courses
And those who sip champagne.
There are those who read the papers
And those who play a game.

There are those who leave a scum line
And those who clean it off.
There are those who hang a door sign
And those who discreetly cough.

There are those who cleanse thrice daily
And those water has rarely seen.
There are those all pale and wrinkly
And those a hose won't clean.

There are those who have an ensuite room
And those with an outside tap.
There are those who shampoo hair to shine
And those who wear a cap.

There are those who need enticing
And those who jump right in.
There are those whose tears start welling
And those with a permanent grin.

All of these are those who divest their clothes
To perform their own ablutions.
For each one of us it's a private must
And we all have our own solutions!

Another Owl and a Pussycat

Another owl and a pussycat went to sea,
Now that was a waste of time,
Neither could float,
There was a hole in the boat
And they sank at half past nine.

The cat looked up through the water above
And thought 'What a stupid bird,
To hope to float
With a hole in the boat
Was really quite absurd.'

They swam underwater for a week and a quarter,
With no sense of time or location,
When they finally made shore
Cat found it cold to the paw,
It was white and huge, a revelation.

Both scrambled ashore, cat lending a paw
To explore this floating mass,
They walked 'round for hours
Finding no trees, shrubs or flowers,
Not even a blade of grass.

The owl asked the cat 'Do you know where we're at,
Do you think we'll be here for a while?'
Cat's shout 'There's a boat'
Brought a lump to his throat
And for the first time the bird had a smile.

As the boat came nearer its name became clearer,
'Till the word 'Titanic' could be seen,
The rest , as they say,
Is just history today,
'Boat hits 'berg and sinks'.

On that day of all days many were saved,
One owl with a cat were but two,
And when they reached home,
They vowed never to roam
In a boat with a hole built for two.

Today those two can be found on a cruise,
Somewhere warm in the sun,
All thoughts of disaster
Are drowned in the laughter,
Of another owl and a cat having fun!

Barking Mad

I bumped into a tree today,
A tree I didn't know,
It barked my crown
And I went down,
From one almighty blow.

Crumpled heap in a twilight daze,
My head both sore and bleeding,
I came around
To the stillest sound,
The tree I swear was smiling.

I lay there pondering my next intent,
The tree, it didn't move,
Just glowered down
At my split crown,
With a lofty attitude.

I thought awhile both long and hard,
Considering too few options,
Chainsaw or axe,
But those thoughts past
In favour of a long-term solution.

Lifting myself onto my feet
To seek my homeward course,
I clutched barked head
Where crown had bled,
The tree showed no remorse.

I thought I caught it watching
As I staggered on my way,
The blow I'd taken
Had left me shaken,
But I vowed to have my day.

I'll wait until each autumn
When its leaves begin to fall,
Then I'll return,
My revenge to earn,
Kick its leaves and burn them all!

Bed and Bored

My brain's kicked in now it's early morn,
Still under sheets keeping bed bugs warm,
I lay quiet and ponder what lies ahead,
Should I ever decide to quit my bed.

I stretch a little then cough a lot,
Smell my breath, but I'd rather not,
Last night's supper has left a taste,
Fish, chips and curry, some going to waste.

I ease both legs from under the sheets,
Odd bed socks still on my feet,
My twisted pyjamas are giving me grief,
I'll take them off if I clean my teeth.

I glance around my litter-strewn room,
It'll need a good cleaning some day soon,
But that's a job for a much earlier start,
I'm still in bed, ain't got the heart.

Bedroom curtains are hanging, the sun pours in,
Sky is true blue and the clouds are thin,
From here it looks such a lovely day,
But the bed's still warm, I might just stay.

The cat went out sometime last night,
By the state it's in there's been a fight,
It's eyeing me with a look forlorn,
Having just thrown up on next door's lawn.

Not a sound around, can I now hear,
No smell of cooking, no cup of cheer,
No post, no papers, no book by bed,
It's the start of a day, I always dread.

I could jump out now and make a move,
Have a shower, get dressed, start my groove,
Or just phone a friend from where I'm lying,
Try acting the fool, pretend I'm dying.

The phone just rings, no-one at home,
No friends I've found to hear my moan,
It's gone mid-day, they're all at work,
I've lazed the morning, what a berk!

I'd best call the boss, complain I'm ill,
It was then I heard my front door bell,
But door's shut tight with no key in lock,
And I'm in the hall in pyjamas and socks.

'Hang on a sec,' I shout at the door,
Spin around and power slide, across the floor,
Straight through the kitchen, colliding with bin,
Exploding the trash all contained therein.

Last night's remains, oil soaked papers and tins,
Egg shells and peelings, sundry odour things,
Head first I stumbled right into it all,
Clouting my nose on the far kitchen wall.

Flying back in a recoil I encounter that bin,
Sending me flying straight back at the sink,
Braking hard on both socks to lessen the crash,
Hit kitchen table and came down in the trash.

As I regain conscious I'm in a strange bed,
People are hovering with masks on their head,
Those masks aren't for germs, just for the smell,
Covering filthy black looks, that much I could tell.

It was to hospital I'm taken, once they'd got in,
Smashing door open and removing that bin,
I've fractured one leg, bust open my nose,
Blackened both eyes and broken four toes.

'Place like a pigsty,' 'in pyjamas and socks,'
A few of the words that went with those looks,
My boss then arrived and gave me the sack,
'Can't use a worker spends all day on his back.'

My neighbour appeared, the one with the lawn,
'I've cleaned it all up but your cat has now gorn,
We've all had it adopted, trust you don't mind,
By a lady with no smell but terribly kind.'

I've no job, no cat and my reputation has gone,
And I've got to lie here 'till the healing is done,
No friends, no telly and nothing to do,
I'm in bed and bored, but that's nothing new!

Down the Plughole

When water leaves the bath you're using,
Where does it go, what are we losing?
Beyond the plug in the bottom of the bath,
What do we know, where goes its path?

Down the pipes and into drains,
Does it stay there if it rains?
Through the manhole, 'round the bends,
Can soap suds last until the end?

Do the soap suds we've created
Come up the bits where drains are grated?
If they do, then, why oh why,
Don't soap suds float and fill the sky?

Down the drains with rats that swim,
Do they dive or just jump in?
If they choose to wash this way,
Do they do it every day?

When your bath water finally stops,
Has it all gone, every drop?
Washing every inch of pipes of clay,
Or does it clog the drain with bits of grey?

If the water leaks along the way,
Does it hang about for another day?
When the rest has passed does it go back in
And flow like mad to catch it up again?

Cascading out at the very end,
Is soapy water ever used again?
If it is, then how do we,
Have so much water in the sea?

Is this soapy water gathered up,
Then pushed down pipes to reach my cup?
Just one thing I now need to know,
Do they clean it all before it goes?

Do they remove the soap, rats and greys,
Before they send it down our ways?
'Cos if they don't, I'll have it said,
I'll bath no more but shower instead!

Duck for Lunch

A duck stepped from the river,
And waddled up to me,
He made no quack
But just lay back,
One wing against a tree.

His other wing he offered
As if my hand to shake,
But what came next
Left me perplexed,
This duck had a point to make.

Wet duck just stood there dripping,
Small puddles at his feet,
He caught my eye
With one long sigh
And then began to speak.

I know that ducks don't talk, they quack,
At least that's what I thought,
But as he cleared his throat
This duck spoke,
To ask me what I'd brought.

I told him 'fish paste sandwiches,
Wild berry pie and flask of tea.'
He just sat down,
There on the ground,
And shared my lunch with me.

He scoffed a lot of the lunch I'd got
And finished off my flask of tea.
Just for a treat
He drank tea sweet,
With not one lump, but three.

It seemed this duck was local,
Never ventured far from home,
But he'd got fed up
With river bed muck
And learnt to speak in human tone.

The duck, by now, was in full flow,
To explain his daily life,
At his nest called home
The young had flown,
Leaving him and just his wife.

The duck began to shiver
With the cold wind around his knees,
I lowered my hat
And there he sat,
Sheltered from the breeze.

He carried on his chatting,
Quite relaxed as I could see,
But when folks came
He'd quack again,
Keeping his talking just for me.

As the day drew on and the light had gone,
The duck stood up to go,
In a light now dim,
I said to him,
'There's one thing I have to know.'

'I understand that you are local,
I understand that you get bored,
But you can walk
And you can talk,
Why don't you fly abroad?'

The duck became embarrassed
And took my offered hand,
'Oh, I can walk
And I can talk
But you don't understand.'

'We neither mind the flying
No matter what the gap,
But if we lost our way
We'd have to stay,
'Cos I can't read a map!'

Early Call

Your English is perfect,
Your manners unique,
I'm aware of an accent,
Right now as we speak.

My phone has been ringing,
All hours night and day,
I've really no interest,
In what you might say.

You start the dog howling,
My wife has now gone,
I wish you'd cease calling,
At all hours to my home.

I have no need of insurance,
New mortgage or loan,
I've got double glazing,
And don't need a phone.

I've no use for your 'Freebie',
Whatever it is,
You get nothing for nothing,
So I'll give it a miss.

If your phone call was local,
You'd be aware of the fact,
That here now it's night-time,
The only thing out is the cat.

Your call could be blocking,
One from a friend,
Someone I'd talk to,
Whose ear I could bend.

I've no wish to be rude,
Impolite, or abrupt,
But your call wasn't asked for,
So be quiet – shut up.

Are you saying I've won it,
Just me, I came top,
Of course I'm delighted,
Oh no – they've hung up!

Eclipsed

Something switched the sun off
Just for a minute or two,
All around was total chaos
'Cos the sun had blown a fuse.

It all went dark at eleven ten
No one was amused,
It did come back just after that
When something tweaked the fuse.

It doesn't happen all that often
And I'm so pleased with that,
But I was caught on holiday
In my 'kiss me quickly' hat.

I was laying getting suntanned
With my lilo going flat,
When suddenly the sun went off
And all the sky went black.

Seagulls began colliding
As day turned into night,
Dogs began their howling,
A truly dreadful sight.

A young lad strolling past me
With water from the sea,
Missed his way on that darkened day
And dropped the lot all over me.

A large chap also stumbled
As he was heading home,
Down with a slap, right on my back,
That chap weighed eighteen stone.

The moms had started searching
For kids they couldn't see,
One ancient gran, took my hand
And started dragging me!

Someone turned the lights on
All along the pier,
Two lads with booze had fallen off
And were searching for their beer.

The lifeboat crew were summoned
With a loud bang in the air,
But the lads paddled in quite safely
'Cos the sea was out so far.

Then the sun began to shine again
And folks had settled down,
With lots of battered seagulls
Seen staggering around the town.

All the moms had got their kids back
And the dogs had ceased to howl,
They took me off in an ambulance
Wrapped up in my hotel towel.

It's only right the sun's off at night
And comes on in the morning,
But in the day it has to stay
Or at least give us some warning!

Father to Son

A tall young lad of eight or nine
Stood between white posts and a washing line,
On his feet, boots well battered,
The large 'one' on his back, all that mattered.

Knowledge passed down from father to son,
Life's sporting curve had already begun,
Diving to his left, leaping to his right
The pair played on in fading light.

'Shoot Dad, shoot' came an alto voice
That in teens would break, he'd have no choice,
'Shoot Dad, shoot' it came again
From a boy that would play in a game among men.

Years went on from ten through teens
With that tall young lad much sought by teams,
Trophies came and medals too,
Too many to count, many more than a few.

Best player awards and invites to trials
As young as fourteen with youthful smiles,
Selections came time after time
For that lad to walk the 'goalies line.'

League clubs called and invited him down,
So many were trialled but no sign of a frown,
Nothing fazed that tall young man
Who played every game as best he can.

Dad played his part in most of the coaching,
Persuading, teaching, shouting and coaxing,
Both regarded those years as time well spent
That started so young and so full of intent.

But the luck that goes with the highest game
Avoided the man, which seemed a shame,
Now looking back, where has it all gone,
That time passed down from father to son?

Feast for Sore Eyes

I had this little budgie,
'Joey' was his name,
I bought another budgie,
And called it 'Joe', the same.

These two would chirp together,
Quite happy on their swing,
But every time I called it,
New budgie, not a thing.

My problem, quite upsetting,
I'm fond of both my 'Joes',
But a budgie that ignores me,
What's the point of one of those?

So now I had a quandary,
What was I to do?
There ain't much meat on budgies,
No point in cooking two.

I would take the two out walking,
In their cage on four new wheels,
Folks would stop and call them,
Not knowing how I'd feel.

Then one day I'd noticed,
Something different 'twixt the two,
New budgies nose was bright and pink,
Old Joey's nose was blue!

It seemed new budgie was a hen,
While old 'Joey' was a cock,
Hen birds ain't called 'Joey',
It must have been to her, a shock.

Immediately I had a plan,
To win new budgies heart,
I'd call the new one 'Josephine',
We'd make a brand new start.

New budgie was delighted,
'Josephine' well fit the bill,
She'd swing and sing her heart out,
With a chirp both loud and shrill.

At night no rest for chirping,
Those two were having a ball,
My eyes though, sore and aching,
No sleep, not a lid would fall.

Day after day it went on,
Near drove me 'round the bend,
Then one day no chirping,
Much quietness did descend.

Creeping close, fearing the worst,
I looked into their cage,
'Josephine' was sat there squatting,
On cage floor like some old sage.

'Joey' started strutting,
Spreading wings and looking pleased,
'Josephine' then proudly raised her head,
Rising slowly from her knees.

Beneath her breast all snug and warm,
'Josephine' had six small eggs,
All that chirping had been courting,
Cage floor became her nest.

In due time all eggs were hatched,
So now my two were eight,
I didn't bother giving names,
I had in mind a plate!

I fed those chicks 'till they were grown,
My two budgies kept on laying,
There'd been no point in cooking two,
But six a time was worth the grill on!

First Thoughts

If I could know while I am young
Of all those things that might go wrong,
That I'd start life on life's bottom wrung,
I doubt I would have bothered!

I'm in this dress they call a gown
It's beyond my feet and goes way down,
I'm the one about to be drowned
By this chap in white with the water!

I'm into crawling, can't yet walk,
Can understand but can't yet talk,
My skin's all smooth like a piece of chalk
And all the ladies want to hug me!

I drink from a bottle with a rubber top
My dad will say 'here comes your pop,'
Bet it's not the same as his night time drop
When he's just like me, both legless!

Here comes my mom and right on time,
With the kit to clean this mess of mine,
I like it best at 'knickerless time,'
Life's surely getting better!

Flushing of 'Aunty Bet'

There once was an outside toilet,
Known to all as 'Aunty Bet'.
Each time you had to flush the thing,
Your feet got soaking wet.

'I'm away outside for a minute,
Off to see old Aunty Bet.'
Everyone knew your destination,
They also knew you'd come back wet.

Behind its door was darkness,
The only light came from outside.
All its walls around were whitewashed,
This was no place to bide.

The cistern head was seven foot high,
Its chain was six foot one.
No point in kneeling for the handle,
Just pull the chain and run.

Some would take its chain outside,
Close the door and pull.
Unless that yank was vertical,
This cistern head stayed full.

Others would climb onto its rim,
To avoid the impending flow.
With water cascading to the floor,
That's the last place they should go.

A knowing few would fill a bucket,
To pour it down the pan.
With exit pipes both slow and small,
That proved a pointless plan.

No one lingered to smoke or read,
Draught, top of door, cured that.
With cold wind blowing around your knees,
'Twas no place to be sat.

High up its walls, a six inch nail,
With newspaper, square torn and pinned.
There was no roll of comfort,
Held aloft with a piece of string.

The wooden seat had long ago,
Gone past what you'd call its 'prime'.
You couldn't say it was comfortable,
Just practical at such a time.

A winter wind would crash the door,
To slam it firmly shut.
If that happened at the flushing,
The water rose above your foot.

In summer times, the door and walls,
Were repainted clean and new.
But still no place to 'stay awhile',
And observe its 'knot hole' view.

The smarter ones, or so they thought,
Would 'outflank' old 'Aunty Bet'.
With plank and bricks, they'd avoid the tricks,
Of a flushing, 'Aunty Bet'.

At times like that, stood or sat,
The clouds would offer rain.
The roof, you see, was holey,
So they still got wet again.

Through those years, 'Aunty Bet' held fears,
For the wise and unaware.
Until they installed a new loo,
Indoors, and up the stairs!

Footloose

You wear a strange outfit,
Painted smile on your face,
A black tear is frozen,
Another, smaller, gives chase.
Large hat with a flower,
Spraying water on all,
Carrying a 'something' filled bucket,
Trying hard not to fall.

No rear end to your trousers,
Check shorts showing through,
Large hanky in pocket,
Sewn in, not to use.
You blast on a hooter,
Like an old car horn,
Large shoes on your feet,
Looking clumsy and worn.

So big, so long,
So wide and so flat,
Laced up at the front,
Large bow 'round the back.
By my guess they would cover,
Thirty inches or more,
Leaving one huge foot print,
With each pace of the floor.

Some things are puzzling,
A few facts I must know,
Do those shoes fit your feet,
Is there room left to grow?
If your toes touch the end,
Are they tightfit or loose,
Where can I buy,
Such ginormous shoes?

If your feet fit all snug,
How about the size of your socks,
Are they handmade to fit,
Can I buy them in shops?
Do they actually cover,
The full length of your feet,
Do toes poke through,
Half covered, but neat?

Your days are spent clowning,
Seems a wonderful life,
But long feet in bed,
Must lift sheets off the wife.
When you try to turn over,
Do sheets cascade to the floor?
I had only one question,
But one hundred thoughts more!

I am desperate for answers
To questions I've asked,
My feet are long too,
Like you, I am cursed.
My fascination remains,
Now your clowning is done,
I will call back tomorrow,
To find where they come from!

Grandads

Grandads don't skip,
Grandads just run,
Grandads are old
But Grandads are fun.

Grandads don't shout,
Grandads just glare,
Grandads are kind
And they mess up your hair.

Grandads don't swim,
Grandads just stand,
Grandads can paddle
If you hold their hand.

Grandads don't argue,
Grandads just fuss,
Grandads buy comics
For children like us.

Grandads don't cycle,
Grandads just mend,
Grandads build castles
With buckets of sand.

Grandads don't sledge,
Grandads just slide,
Grandads will find us
Wherever we hide.

Grandads don't cook,
Grandads just eat,
Grandads wear slippers
Outside in the street.

Grandads don't sing,
Grandads just hum,
Grandads will chase us
So we can have fun.

Grandads don't look,
Grandads just see,
Grandads build houses
Way up in a tree.

Grandads don't learn,
Grandads just know,
Grandads will miss us
Wherever we go.

Grandads don't show it,
Grandads just care,
Grandads need loving.
Whoever they are!

Grandmas

Grandmas are forever,
That's how is seems.
Grandmas are mothers
With brand new dreams.

Grandmas have children
Now married and flown.
Grandma's new babies,
As loved as her own.

Grandmas like children,
Clean nappies, small nose.
Grandmas blow bubbles
On fingers and toes.

Grandmas have love
In abundance to spare.
Grandmas hide sweets,
In pockets to share.

Grandmas can teach
The small ones of life.
Grandmas protect,
Those small ones from strife.

Grandmas will listen,
To tales large and small.
Grandmas will kiss,
The scratch of a fall.

Grandmas replace,
Tears with a smile.
Grandmas can feel,
The pain of a child.

Grandmas will bathe,
The baby again.
Grandmas just know,
The love to be gained.

Grandmas will push,
A buggy for miles.
Grandmas find pleasure,
In the faintest of smiles.

Grandmas can talk,
In a baby's own words.
Grandmas will listen,
For a cry to be heard.

Grandmas will watch,
Her new babies growing.
Grandmas are wise,
All loving, all knowing.

Growing Old Disgracefully

I've a need to grow old disgracefully,
Learn to fart and belch when I please.
Create my own sonic boom
In a crowded room
And blame it on too many greens.

I've a need to grow old disgracefully,
Do away with a belt, feel at ease.
Have loud braces that twang
Holding trousers that hang,
With the crutch in a knot at my knees.

I've a need to grow old disgracefully,
Join Darby and Joan down the hall.
Go away on the trips,
Eat vinegar soaked chips
And burp at the belle of the ball.

I've a need to grow old disgracefully,
Keep pigeons in a loft out the back.
Let them all out
When there's washing about,
'Till the neighbours call 'round with a cat.

I've a need to grow old disgracefully
Wear a vest with buttons and sleeves.
Have a tee shirt on top
Of some long ago pop,
Like the Quo, the Slade or Queen.

I've a need to grow old disgracefully,
Hoard footballs that land on my lawn.
Cuss at the kids,
Bang my own dustbin lids
From sunset 'till way past dawn.

I've a need to grow old disgracefully,
Eat meals off a plate edged with rust.
It will never get washed
Or even wiped with a cloth
But scraped clean with a soft piece of crust.

I've a need to grow old disgracefully,
Forget to ease up the zip when I've peed.
There'll be stains down the front
That will dry in the sun,
Carefully nurtured for others to see.

I've a need to grow old disgracefully,
Fire my chimney to lift out the mess.
Just where it fell
I could always tell
By the sootmarks on a newly-washed dress.

I've a need to grow old disgracefully,
Whip my teeth out whenever I please.
Picking them clean
With sharp match or pin
Then a polish along the length of my sleeve.

I've a need to grow old disgracefully,
Button my old coat two holes out of line.
With one sandal and shoe
Down the pub for a brew,
On my own 'till past closing time.

I've a need to grow old disgracefully,
Grow whiskers with food bits entwined.
In my galvanised tub
On bathday each month,
Bit picking would help pass the time.

I've a need to grow old disgracefully,
Stacking used pots and pans 'till gone hard.
When needing another,
Without too much bother,
Hose down what I need on the yard.

I've a need to grow old disgracefully,
Do those things posh folks never do.
Go on a giant mud slide,
Park a car on its side,
Take my snuff in an outside loo.

I've a need to grow old disgracefully,
Lady luck has provided the chance.
I've come up on the pools
Now I can act the old fool,
On my yacht in the south of France!

Home Made

Gone are those days of home-made crumble,
Guaranteed to silence any 'tummy rumble',
With custard hot and running smooth,
An extra portion, no way you'd move.

Where are those pies that grandma made,
Straight from the oven to cool in the shade,
Piping hot and burning fingers,
It's amazing how that memory lingers.

Those rabbit stews that simmered for days,
All veggies in, nothing to waste,
Breakfast, dinner and even tea,
There was never enough, not for me.

Bacon cut thick from the corner shop,
Fat 'round the edge that burnt at the top,
Chomped in a butty or egged on a plate,
Breakfasts like that lasted right through the day.

Sat warm by the oven while a cake was baking,
The very smell set bellies aching,
Daren't open the door while the cake was in,
But 'bags first slice,' still hot from the tin.

Boiled eggs with faces, painted on,
Nothing to frighten, just for fun,
Yolks, deep orange, fresh from the hen,
Food tasted different, way back then.

Jams that were stirred for hours at the stove,
Much patience required as each stone was removed,
Bottled in jars kept from other uses,
Then heaped on butter and new bread slices.

Roast beef on a Sunday if we had the cash,
Fresh dug tatties with carrots, horseradish, a dash,
Yorkshire pud to the side with a hot gravy cover,
Plates all polished, nothing left over.

Jam roly poly with syrup on top,
Watch it slide to the bottom and cover the lot,
Those spoons were huge, that's how it seemed,
Puddings, gi-normous, in those days of dreams.

Semolina and sago coloured with jam,
Rice puddings, home-made, straight from the pan,
Porridge and pancakes, a day's early start,
A full pint of milk for the young at heart.

Ham hocks boiling, cauliflowers too,
Sprouts and cabbage creating a 'phew',
Windows wide open right through the year,
Fresh air a blessing, central heating, not here!

All sorts of fruits eaten fresh from the tree,
No washing required before given to me,
No pesticides used 'to protect the fruit,'
Then came the ministry, the man in a suit.

Regulations imposed by the E.E.C,
Nobody mentioned past dangers to me,
Less sugar and fat, no salt on the dinner,
Small shops losing, big stores the winner.

The ASDAs, Tescos, Sainsburys and all,
No longer 'the shop', now 'the food hall,'
Once we ate fresh and straight to the pan,
Now it's microwaved, once free of the can.

Taking the time to reflect again,
Did childhood mealtimes cause me pain?
But for the pennies they all claim we save,
My poor old grandma would turn in her grave!

I Can't See Me

I can see my arms, legs and feet,
See my belly, but not my seat.
I can see my nose from either side,
See my own top lip, if I lift it high.

Can't see my ears, face or hair,
Can't see my eyes, to see I'm there.
Can't see my chin, neck or back,
To see it's clean, grimed or black.

My eyes are blue, or so I'm told,
My face is lined, so I could be old.
Below my chin, my skin is smooth,
How come my face feels full of grooves?

I look in a mirror and see a face,
It could be mine, it's in my place.
I recognise my arms, legs and feet,
Never seen that face, out on the street.

No reflection feels like the face I've got,
I'm in 3D, the mirror is not.
I've got lumps, but the reflection's flat,
I see two eyes, both looking back.

Does the reflection see me, or do I see it,
When it stands, I do, when it sits, I sit.
How do I know that face is mine,
Just because it's on a body like mine?

If I can't see, my front, my face,
I can only imagine what's in its place.
Is my reflection true, if it's what I see,
How do I know if I can't see me?

Illuminating

I sat down by a lady I barely knew
In dark blue coat and bright red shoes,
On her head, and too large to mention,
Sat a hat of extreme dimension.

The hat was covering all of her hair,
Most of her face and half of the chair,
Being confronted with all of that
I thought to ask her about the hat.

Curiosity getting the better of me
I sought her attention with a cough or three,
My interest aroused by this awesome sight,
I begged to enquire in a manner, polite.

'Excuse me ma'am, but I have to ask,
Are you wearing that hat as a punishment task,
Is someone paying, do you do it for free,
Is it more of a bet, it's sure puzzling me?'

The lady laughed near fit to burst,
Unpinned the hat to show me the worst,
From a salon she'd come having coloured her hair,
With the colour changing even as I stared.

First it turned red, then it turned blue,
Changing again to a purple hue,
The colours unstable, that became clear,
No need to be close, no need to be near.

It seemed her salon had made a boob,
Too many colours from so many tubes,
All the blending made the colour unstable,
To tell what it was, no one was able.

The lady asked me after a while,
'Do you prefer any colour in any one style,
I'm due at lunch with friends at three,
Do you think they'll notice the changing me?'

By the time she'd finished I was laughing aloud,
The noise and the hair had gathered a crowd,
The lady, unstressed, was modelling now,
Back and forth, taking a bow.

I put my mind to solving her problem,
A task like this doesn't come too often,
But then it arrived, that inspiration,
I knew where to place this female sensation.

We jumped onto a bus then onto a train,
Straight onto a tram in pouring rain,
To arrive in Blackpool in fading light
Where they light up her hair on Saturday night.

If you crave to see this amazing attraction,
Visit the 'mile' with its illuminations,
She's up there connected to mains type power
With hair colour changing, hour after hour!

Itchy Feet

I was strolling slowly on a pebbled beach,
When I had an itch on both my feet.
Off came my shoes,
Off came my socks,
Leaving me barefoot on the rocks.

I scratched one foot and then the other,
'Till both were sore and red all over.
But no relief,
Despite the scratching,
And now both feet had started bleeding.

I looked around and to my surprise,
Both my socks were on the tide.
One shoe had gone,
The other going,
Just where I was, no way of knowing.

With the sea now lapping at both my feet,
I thought it best, beat a quick retreat.
Away from the beach,
Above the water,
Up I went to a safer quarter.

Using hands and feet to aid my climb,
I failed to note the passing time.
Feet still bleeding,
So were hands,
I wished I'd never seen those sands.

By now the light had left the day,
And I no longer saw my way.
Above the beach,
Safe from drowning,
A large sand hole to stop me falling.

Feet, by now, had ceased their itching,
But, like my hands, had lost all feeling.
Tearing shorts and shirt,
To bind them tight,
I settled down to a cold dark night.

Right through I lay in that sandy place,
No hand to see before my face.
Stomach rumbling,
Need the loo,
Just lying still, nothing else to do.

Morning came and to my surprise,
Short green grass before my eyes.
'Fore' I heard,
That fateful shout,
When a bright-white ball caught me a clout.

I leapt erect in that sandy hole,
Feeling less a man and more a mole.
Two lumps appeared,
The size of eggs,
One on each foot, buckling legs.

I danced around in awesome pain,
That itching gone had come again.
Cloth strips off
To view the bleeding,
When a toff appeared and started ranting.

'I say old chap this isn't on,
One's bunker's no place to catch the sun.
Dress code you know,
Dashed awful tight,
Underpants won't do, dreadful sight.'

It seemed last night I'd reached the top,
Climbed those rocks, a fearful drop,
Spent the night,
Both safe and sound,
Right on a golf course, part way around.

I viewed below that pebbled beach,
With socks and shoes now out of reach.
Cut my hands,
Feet as well,
Saw his clubs, thought 'what the hell'.

Took his bag and held it high,
Above my head, a clear blue sky.
Below my feet,
Morning dew,
Sent me sliding, bag came too!

Down I went back to that beach,
Struck by clubs within my reach.
Now black and blue
And scratched all over,
Fell into water, without much bother.

Safe and sound I stood up straight,
Soaked body now all full of hate.
Gathered clubs,
Bag as well,
And chucked the lot in the morning swell.

A lesson here for those who stroll,
Along a beach near water cold.
If an itch appears
On both your feet,
Stand in the water, it works a treat!

Jim the Wing – A Down to Earth Guy!

I'd just dropped off,
Woke up with a cough,
When I heard the faintest sound.
It was a tapping I'd heard,
But that was absurd,
I'm six miles above the ground.

I looked all about,
But didn't look out,
The blind at my window was down.
Couldn't trace that tap
From where I was sat,
And my face, by now, had a frown.

Looking all around,
Above and then down,
No hint of a tap did I find.
My attention regained
As it started again,
From behind my drawn window blind.

This began bothering me,
That was plain to see,
I'm on a jet returning from Spain!
With no place to hide
On a plane's outside,
What could be tapping my pane?

Curiosity aroused,
Way above the clouds,
I asked if I was alone.
All started laughing,
None heard the tapping,
'Relax, you'll soon be at home.'

It was then that I heard
Just eight English words,
Above the drone of the jets.
'My name is Jim,
Can I come in?'
Frightened me near to death.

This just cannot be,
It can't happen to me,
Am I mad or going insane.
Gathering my wits,
I turned in my seat,
And opened the blind to my pane.

Out there on the wing
Was this chap called Jim,
Strapped on with an old bungee cord.
His hair, frost white,
His rucksack open, but tight,
From him, those eight urgent words.

As my panic set in
Jim started to grin,
Someone had noticed his plight.
The bungee was fraying,
Jim wouldn't be staying,
He'd be losing his place on this flight.

I called for the steward
Who then rushed forward,
Returning with captain and crew.
All gathered around,
Now catching the sound,
And the sight, all crazy but true.

With all the weight on my side,
Jim started to slide,
As bodies forced the plane wing to dip.
Where Jim was going,
We'd no way of knowing,
Bungee parted, throwing Jim off the tip.

With Jim now gone,
We carried on,
Our captain reporting the loss.
Met as we landed,
We were all grounded,
Filling uncountable forms for the police.

Two days after that,
The press reported the facts,
Good fortune had saved our chap Jim.
He feared, as he fell,
That he was heading for hell,
As he slipped off the tip of our wing.

It seems he'd descended
With open rucksack upended,
To the top of a hot air balloon.
With frayed bungee wrapped 'round,
All fell to the ground,
Close to a choir thrown well out of tune.

Jim had landed in Wales,
Somewhere in the hills,
On Anglesey's beautiful isle.
Folks were given a fright,
At this unusual sight,
But the choir soon restored their lost smiles.

Jim, on the same day,
Decided to stay,
Joined the choir after learning to fly.
Now known across Wales
Because of this tale,
As 'Jim the wing', a down to earth guy.

Mavis Upchuck – A T.V. Child

Little Mavis Upchuck was a moody sort of child,
She seldom laughed, never joked, and rarely ever smiled.

'She could mope for England,' her dad was oft to say,
As she stayed at home, sat on her own, watching T.V. every day.

Mavis never skipped an advert, let alone her favourite soap,
T.V., it seemed, held all her dreams, Mavis spent each day in hope.

Her school work didn't hide it, her ratings, far from good,
But Mavis had ambitions, way beyond those small girls should.

Mavis saw her future as clear as a bright blue day,
It didn't seem, to her a dream, but true in every way.

She knows just where she's heading, the how, the why and when,
Mavis saw it happening as soon as she turned ten.

That big ten came and went again with Mavis undeterred,
'I'll just plod on, along this road I'm on, my future is assured'.

Birthdays came and birthdays went, right past all her teens,
With Mavis watching more T.V., fixated with her dreams.

As Mavis crept past thirty, her T.V. went on the blink,
No programmes there to guide her, now Mavis had to think.

A situation most could cope with, but Mavis had lost a friend,
But she recalled a T.V. advert for someone who could mend.

Now life is seldom written, along a narrow track,
Most folks find, that over time, blue skies come from black.

And so it was for Mavis, her change in life appeared,
A nice young man, and on his van, 'Busted T.V.'s all repaired.'

Mavis took, one long hard look, at a vision standing there,
Overalls pristine, a smile that beamed, the blackest of short black
hair.

'You called me ma'am I've brought my van, tools are all inside,
Just point me at the T.V., I'll see what I can find.'

Mavis stood there gobsmacked with the broadest of a smile,
But smiling was to Mavis, the gold for the Olympic mile.

Mavis had never tried it, but this smile, it just appeared,
It made her face just radiate, a thing she'd always feared.

The more she stood there smiling, the more she realised,
That, thirty years of T.V. was nothing like real life.

Mavis sat the young man down, his name was Arthur More,
But friends of his, all in the 'bis', called him 'Arfa Mo'.

'I'll have it up and running, fixed in Arfa Mo,
There it is, what bust is fixed, Miss Upchuck, give it a go!'

Mavis turned it on and off and paid the man in cash,
'I'll make for us a cup of tea if you don't have to dash'.

Cups of tea turned into suppers on more than one occasion,
Mavis and her Arthur, were hooked beyond all reason.

They had so much in common, above all else, T.V.,
That it soon became accepted, they were meant to be.

No Mavis mopes, but laughs and jokes, a change deep and dramatic,
The old T.V., no longer seen, but shoved up in the attic.

Things all went fine and in due time, More-Upchucks came to be,
No moody kids with T.V. lids, but a fun-filled family.

So, if you choose, your life to lose, sitting watching the T.V.,
You may not click as Mavis did, but still be there way past fifty!

My Long Time Friend

I lost my long time friend today,
Someone I'd known for years.
I wasn't there when he passed away,
Lord, let him see my tears.

The friend I've lost was a gentle man,
Large in heart and stature.
With time for all right through the pain,
That was his very nature.

A man whose ear he'd always lend,
His time was mine for sharing.
My troubled thoughts he'd help to mend,
With a word and so much caring.

He always had a smile in place,
Beneath his shock white hair.
True friendship beamed out from his face,
Lighting up his corner chair.

White working apron to start his day,
Glasses to the tip of his nose.
But now he's gone it's sad to say,
He won't be needing those.

I still see my friend but with furrowed brow
As I will for all my years,
I'll miss him then as I miss him now,
Lord, let him see my tears.

Nosey or What?

Folks all think I'm nosey,
But I'll have you know I'm not,
It's just that I, have a need to know,
What other folks have got.
That keeps this body busy,
Passing on a tale or two,
Not that I would ever gossip,
About the likes of you.

I trust my friends immensely,
I'm sure they do the same,
I would never spread their business,
To an unknown 'what's-his-name'.
Not unless the same could offer,
A juicy word or two,
Then it's quite O.K. to swop them yours,
For something new on you.

From where I crouch in my front room,
I can view the street,
Fixed angles to my mirrors,
All set to work a treat.
Should I spot someone, sneaking past,
Who may have a tale to share,
I'm down the path to my front gate,
With twenty yards to spare.

On occasion my view can be impaired,
By a vehicle parked outside,
I then berate the drivers,
And insist they move aside.
When they see that I mean business,
Most of them comply,
They understand that I'm not nosey,
But I do need a clear view spy.

Most folks I can encourage,
To pass on their news to me,
The one or two that don't reply,
I rubbish them for free.
I'm not an evil person,
'A gossip', is not my claim,
I need to pass on knowledge,
It gives my life an aim.

Folks do behave all coy-like,
Whenever I'm about,
They rarely come out and tell me,
I have to coax it out.
It cannot be that they don't trust me,
I epitomise discretion,
No point in reporting, what I've heard,
To someone who won't listen.

Sometimes I don't have all the facts,
So bits I will invent,
It's always done with an honest face,
And full of good intent.
I would rarely start a rumour,
To purposely upset,
All those I've ever started,
Are the best I've heard of yet.

I can only enlarge on gossip,
If I have the basic facts,
Unfound rumours have a way,
Of quickly circling back.
No point to self embarrass,
Should it all rebound on me,
I'd rather see you squirming,
Without knowing who it might be.

There's just one type in my life,
For whom I have no time,
It's those who spread the word on me,
They can be so unkind.
It can't be right to backstab me,
In such a way I can't reply,
I'm a person to be trusted,
I'm your friend, now would I lie?

Old Fashioned – Millionaire

I'm just an old fashioned chap,
With a flattened woollen cap,
Baler twine, to stop my trousers falling.
I'm just the old fashioned kind,
With a sharp eccentric mind,
I'm an old fashioned – millionaire.

The old fashioned house in which I live,
Has darkened thatch that's like a sieve,
A wooden fence, that has more gaps than palings.
With dead roses 'round the door,
Worn out carpets on the floor,
No-one, would ever guess, that I've got savings.

My old car that I still use,
Is now red rust but was cerise,
More holes, than I would care to mention.
I wouldn't swop my Cadillac,
For something else that's just as naff,
I still use it every week, to fetch my pension.

All the money I've got stashed,
Helps me pay my way with cash,
Millionaire seeking ladies, needn't bother calling.
One other thing that 'gets my goat',
Is messy oil on a five pound note,
They all get cleaned, and then a careful ironing.

Folks around all think I'm mean,
'Cos I like my money clean,
It's just me, with cash, I'm extra careful.
There's no point in wasting time,
Hanging washing on the line,
Laundered notes, a much more cheerful eyeful.

I have a spade and a fork,
That I use for the garden work,
My 'Earthy Kit', is what they're known to me as.
They just help to pass the time,
With cleaned notes hanging on the line,
And to be sure, 'lightfingers' keep on passing.

No-one knows where the cash comes from,
But I'll tell them if I'm drunk,
About a suitcase, I dug up in my garden.
I took the suitcase home,
To my surprise, when all alone,
Full of notes, and not a single used one.

I've invested wisely over years,
Made my fortune, it appears,
More cash than I could dream of spending.
If the owner comes to call,
For a suitcase and wherewithal,
I know nothing, and would say 'you must be joking'.

All of this just came about,
When my 'Earthy Kit' were out,
To lift some spuds, from where they were a'growing.
Now my gardens concrete,
With towering trees and wooden seat.
And a brook, that like my money, keeps a'flowing.

The thing in life I like the best,
Is lifting spuds in shorts and vest,
After dark, not casting any shadows.
And the noise I think excels,
Is the sound each spud expels
As they drop, plop, plop, into the barrow.

I'm just an old fashioned chap,
With a flattened woollen cap,
Spend my days in sunshine, in my garden, on my back.
I'm just an old fashioned chap,
Who barrows spuds into a sack,
I'm just an old fashioned – millionaire!

Our Kid

They've put the lid on 'our kid',
Placed gently to rest,
Laid him out nicely
In long johns and vest.

'No fuss' was his wish,
Right there in his will,
No need for a shroud,
Far side of the hill.

The service was simple,
No-one else came,
You can't tell folks,
When you haven't their name.

Our friends were aplenty,
All over the place,
Most would recall,
'Our kid' by his face.

The scars of the past,
All told a tale,
Etched deep in his face,
Turned big men to pale.

Up hill and down dale,
A welcome from all,
For 'our kid' and me,
Whenever we'd call.

He took kindly to folks,
But they not to him,
He didn't like bathing
And then there's the Gin.

Our clothes, all borrowed,
Off someone's back line,
All different places,
But one at a time.

Tight fisted we weren't,
Just careful maybe,
Working our way,
'Our kid' and me.

Odd jobs that we found,
All kept us employed,
Paying our way,
Sharing our joys.

Ever light on our feet,
In case we should run,
Not getting caught,
All part of the fun.

Us neither got wed,
Married couples can't roam,
Roots start to grow,
Once needing a home.

Ladies were many,
Flirtations, a score,
With futures encroaching,
'twas swift through the door.

Adventures we had,
Scrapes, more than a few,
One looked for the other,
You took on the two.

But now that he's gone,
I'm out on my own,
Will I settle down,
Or maybe just roam?

'Our kid' wouldn't mind,
His time has been,
It's my time now,
To follow our dream.

So, I'll carry one bag,
Instead of the two,
Strolling straight on,
To adventures anew.

Deep in my mind,
There's a place for 'our kid',
The one that he had,
Before they screwed down the lid.

Some things will change,
As I roam on my own.
'Our kid's' up there somewhere,
But he ain't on the phone.

I know he'll be watching,
Envious maybe,
So I'll carry right on,
For 'our kid' and me.

Our Nature

Deep blacks of the night,
Blue greens in the sea,
White surf tops that fade,
Inches from feet.

Silver pin dots of stars,
Red rays of the sun,
Grey whites on the moon,
Rose pinks in a dawn.

Gold shades of autumn,
All once had been green,
The full spectrum of rainbows,
Once raindrops have been.

The yellows of butter,
From the whiteness of milk,
The dark depths of oceans,
Clear crystal once spilt.

Sheet white of lightning,
From clouds of dark grey,
Blue skies resuming,
Streaked with travellers ways.

The wet black of marble,
Soft sands on a beach,
Hard colours of timber,
Fine hairs on a peach.

Bold colours of life,
On flowers, fish and birds,
So vivid, so subtle,
Leaves man lost for words.

A deep purple of rage,
The envy of green,
A greyness for age,
Some cover with cream.

Many colours of skin,
But all pink inside,
No blueness of blood,
For crimsons to hide.

Dark ages of war,
True softness to peace,
The glowing with joy,
Blue sadness of grief.

The colourless air,
Untouched, never found,
The passing of time
Without making a sound.

The warmth from the sun,
All air free to breath,
Earths food to sustain,
Our nature's true gifts!

Our Time

As each life draws nearer to its close,
Just when it will be, no-one knows,
No king or queen, no new-born too,
Has that knowledge, has a clue.

As time winds down do we spare a thought,
For all those things we could have sought,
About our plans we should have tasted,
Has the time we've had all been wasted?

Did we stroll through life just passing time,
Or did we leave a mark and say, 'that's mine,'
Did we just sit back to watch others create,
Leave it for later, have we left it too late?

Has the time we've had, often rendered pleasure,
On rare occasions, did we find a treasure,
Have we yet to achieve our life long aim,
Of power, glory, fortune or fame?

We all have dreams, but not all react,
Those who do seem to head the pack,
Is the route we follow, down to our own life plan,
Or is life mapped out, from its own day one?

Can we vary that route, alter its course,
Or is destiny preset, for better, for worse,
When we reach a fork, in our life time route,
What instinct decides, to the left or right?

Does our nature vary, from our own day one,
Has it been predetermined, before we've begun,
Are we born to be lucky, to achieve, or to lose,
In the time we're allotted, do we have time to choose?

Can we look back on life, no matter how long?
Encourage what's right, correct what's wrong,
Vary our route, from life experience earned,
Or is the answer preset, whatever we've learned?

From our moment of birth, time is ebbing away,
There's no guarantee, how long we can stay,
Then, what we achieve, or leave as our mark,
Will we do it with vision, or spend 'our time' in the dark?

Pets Not Welcome

A bird flew through my window,
Laying 'shite' all around the room.
I went out back,
Dragged in the cat,
A dust pan and a broom.

The cat went true ballistic,
The bird didn't seem to care.
It just let fly,
Some caught my eye,
The rest, all in my hair.

The cat flew up the curtains,
Almost to the top.
Sliding down with claws
'til it hit the floor,
My curtains, torn and shot.

The bird flew past a mirror,
Just above my ornament shelf.
Liking what it saw,
It did it three times more,
Just to admire its feathered self.

Bric-a-brac flew in all directions,
Most of it was smashed.
Some hit the cat,
Who wasn't having that,
My room was getting trashed.

The cat took to the pelmet,
Leaping from a chair.
Falling chair caught me,
Across both legs and knees,
And the bird re-shite my hair.

The cat reached a conclusion,
With the chair flat on its back.
With no way down,
And bird still flying 'round,
It leapt off to attack.

Missing the bird completely,
Fish tank absorbed cat's fall.
With tidal wave created,
My fish had all migrated,
Across the floor and up the wall.

I struggled back onto my feet,
Again colliding with the chair.
The next I knew,
I'm soaked right through,
More shite and fish in hair.

At this the bird stopped flying,
The cat came to a halt.
My fish, now on the ground,
Just flapping around,
No way it was their fault.

Each eyed me with the strangest look,
The bird and cat uniting.
Both had allied,
As my fish they spied,
Bringing a cease-fire to their fighting.

The bird then took off to my left,
The cat went to my right.
I swung my broom,
All around the room,
My fish weren't there to bite!

The dustpan I then lowered,
To retrieve my fish collection.
Safely gathering all,
I took another fall,
Across the chair that I'd just flattened.

Dustpan flew into the air,
Scattering fish in all directions.
The cat and bird,
Each took one third,
Leaving me the rest of my collection.

The cat and bird both legged it,
Through the window it came in.
I hurled the broom,
Across the room,
Striking tank with fish therein.

Needless to say, on such a day,
Remaining fish did not survive.
The tank was smashed,
As down it crashed,
I was lucky to be alive.

Rushing to the open window,
All my frustration I gave vent.
Then a patrolling cop,
Screeched to a stop,
My arrest, his sole intent.

They took me off in handcuffs,
To the big house full of police.
They became alarmed,
I'd caused animals harm,
Charging me with disturbing the peace.

I have to say, that to this day,
No more pets are ever welcome.
With my home all dried,
And windows locked inside,
There's no way I'm getting 'shite on'!

Phone Man

Driving sedately along the motorway,
I spotted a motorist blocking my way.
With one hand on his wheel,
The other to phone,
His driving erratic, car starting to roam.

Now, I'm a driver of patience immense,
But this behaviour was making me tense,
Should I fall back,
Avoid all confrontation,
Or just overtake with gesticulation?

I closed the gap to less than a metre,
A quick flash of my lights at his rear view mirror,
Tooted my horn,
His attention to gain,
He carried on phoning, this bloke was a pain!

Drove a bit closer, headlights full on,
Blasted my horn to the beat of a drum.
This one is deaf,
Or blind as well,
I began shouting then started to yell.

Not one scrap of notice does he appear to take,
I'm becoming frustrated, starting to shake.
He carries on phoning,
But glancing my way,
Keep it up son, make my day!

'Enough of this', I tell myself,
His driving is lethal, affecting my health.
I pull out to pass,
Forget indicating,
Three vehicles behind commence heavy braking.

I'm surrounded by fools but 'phone man' is mine,
I draw alongside, my speed eighty nine.
One hand to my ear,
The other a fist,
It was then that I noticed something I'd missed.

A word on his car, blue lights on top,
This was no 'phone man', this was a cop.
Blown it big time,
Mega trouble I'm in,
'Phone man' with three stripes, starting to grin.

'Pull the car over, hard shoulder will do,'
No words did I hear, but I just knew.
Tried to slow down,
Comply with his wish,
Collided with 'phone man', twenty car crash.

Now I'm up in court for dangerous driving,
Twenty car write off but all drivers surviving.
I'm going down,
'Phone man', no phone,
'That cop was a set up,' I heard myself moan.

Three months I got with a twelve month ban,
Insurance sky high, just covers a van.
Acceleration restricted,
A nice steady fifty,
Ignore all the 'phone men' and blokes looking shifty.

I suppose in a way, there's just me to blame,
But no 'phone man' will con me ever again.
I'll drive more sedately,
Cruise my way home,
Oh, hang on a sec, there goes my phone!

Pigeons Came First

Before mobile phones there were pigeons,
Kept in a loft, up steps, outside.
Fixed tight to each leg,
And much smaller than eggs,
Two tubes with rolled paper inside.

No need for those masts down the highway,
Polluting the air with their vibes.
The pigeon just flew,
To someone you knew,
With a note on the paper you'd scribed.

Each pigeon was trained to fly in the rain,
Through wind, snow, sunshine or storm.
Not requiring 'lectronics,
And its own speed subsonic,
Just sustained on water and corn.

In wars they were used, to carry the news,
Flying low, unseen, and with speed.
You can't use the phone,
With the batteries gone,
A pigeon is all that you'd need.

Phone calls can be intercepted,
Overheard, by non-friends and unknown.
But a pigeon just flew
To a friend, back to you,
Undisturbed, discreet and alone.

In this day and age, what causes a rage,
Are those with a mobile at face.
In a car, train or tram,
With their own traffic jam,
Or a restaurant invading my space.

A pigeon can have other uses,
They're relaxing to sit and watch fly.
Their bobbing of heads,
When using both legs,
Fascinates the unaware eye.

A pigeon would be my own preference,
No hidden charges are lurking within.
Getting too plump to fly,
They go well in a pie,
Old mobiles just go in the bin!

Questions and Answers

'Is my backside too big for this stool,
Or is the seat it supports, way too small.
If I should initiate a wobble,
Will it cause me some trouble,
Can you catch me if I should fall?'

'Your backside is causing much consternation,
Your fear of falling, one can well understand.
If indeed you should fall,
One could be crushed at the wall,
One would rather you let go of one's hand.'

'If I promise to fall, away from the wall,
Is there somewhere soft I can land.
If my size proves too much,
Will I come down in a ruck,
Are you sure I can't hold onto your hand?'

'Your softest place is below the back of your face,
It has the look of inflation by pump.
You may just be alright,
If you leap off, take flight,
One can only suggest you go jump.'

'If I do let go and strike the floor here below,
Are you sure it will take all of the strain.
If I should crash clean through,
Those below might then sue,
Will I bruise or incur much pain?'

'From a one metre height, you will look a sight,
If you should manage to land backside first.
One doubts you'll crash through,
But if you do, it's the loo,
So your embarrassment, not pain, will be worst.'

'The predicament I'm in, is no source of fun,
I can see that you're no help at all.
How can you just stand,
And not offer your hand,
I've this feeling I'm just going to fall.'

'One would suggest, get a grip, stop quivering your lip,
There's no way you can sit there all day.
The stool will start breaking,
With your volume it's taking,
And if it hasn't already, it well may.'

'I think you could be more understanding,
It's the stool, not backside, that's not right.
You'd have thought they'd provide,
Stools that backsides can't hide,
At my rear I must look a sight.'

'From the side and the back, you've skin that looks slack,
Giving a fullness of overhang droop.
The stool has a seat,
For the small and petite,
With no provision for containment or scoop.'

'That's it, that's it, I'll find somewhere to fit,
I'll not be the 'butt' of your fun.
My backside is mine,
And I like it just fine,
Look out floor below, here I come!'

The thought of this tale, is that, those who prevail,
Find more answers to questions than some.
If the seat is too small,
Find another, that's all,
Other answers are out there, find one!

Quitting the Nicotine!

I've given up the dreaded weed,
Done away with smoking fags,
No more coughing in the rain,
Just to have another drag.

Said I'd do it, loads of times,
Always thought there'd be no problem,
This standing out in wind and rain,
Has happened once too often.

You fidget, smoke, while getting soaked,
With a 'ciggy', soft and limp,
It takes a pack for just one hack,
Once damp they're in the bin.

I often note, that folks who don't,
Are offended by my smoke,
Barring smokers all, from every hall,
Goes way beyond a joke.

It's not allowed in pubs and clubs,
No inhaling while you're dining,
Can't even light up on a bus,
No wonder I've stopped smiling.

The 'room' they provide, that 'thing' outside,
Four poles and a canvas roof,
Lets wind howl through, rainwater too,
The sly don't use it, that's the truth.

They'll take a pew, locked in the loo,
Light up, ignore the ban,
In no time at all, alarm bells bawl,
Flush the whole lot down the pan.

My pledge will work, I'm sure of that,
Life's pleasure, all but done,
But I feel good, at least, I should,
Now my cravings almost gone.

I feel relaxed, no shakes or lapse,
It's just gone ten to two,
I stopped at one, my last fag's gone,
Can I cadge a drag off you?

Redundant

Was working once,
Now I'm not,
Made redundant,
Lost the plot.

Job for life,
So I thought,
Grafted hard,
Came to nought.

No time off,
Not even sick,
Loved my job,
Must be thick.

Cut our pay,
Save the works,
Closed it down,
Management berks.

Sold the house,
Car as well,
Upset the kids,
I could tell.

Moved away,
Different place,
Self employed,
Smile on face.

Took on partner,
Old work mate,
Known for years,
Feeling great.

Work all hours,
Every day,
Pulled large job,
Heavy pay.

Firm went bust,
No invoice met,
All laid off,
Worst day yet.

Mope all day,
Upset the wife,
Bank foreclosing,
Such is life.

One fiver left,
Found a shop,
Lottery ticket,
Blew the lot.

Saturday night,
Watch the draw,
Power went off,
How much more.

Partner phoned,
He'd won a mill,
Partying started,
Pay all bills.

Cheered me up,
His good luck,
Kept the kids,
My wife he took.

Moved to Spain,
Kids and me,
Love the sun,
By the sea.

No one knows,
Until today,
Where from my cash,
To pay our way.

Winning numbers,
I had too,
Didn't tell wife,
But kids all knew!

Sheltered

Water lapping against the hull,
Lonely call of a grounded gull.
Wind rattling haliyards against the mast,
Anchor down and holding fast.
Sails all furled then stowed away,
Boat ship-shape for another day.
Deck all clear, leave nothing loose,
Ride the swell and feel its pulse.
Shelter found to evade the storm,
Accept delay perhaps 'till dawn.
Nature will have her way tonight,
Should be ours by early light.
Out there the waves with deepening troughs,
In shelter here it's calm enough.
No rest tonight, stay wide awake,
Hear the noise the wind can make.
Long hours on watch, always aware,
Should we drift there's danger there.
Given time the storm will fade,
Come the dawn, receding shade.
Sea will calm and we sail on,
Some miles lost but no harm done.
Nature demands our deep respect,
Sea and wind her biggest threat.
Like the tide the wind can turn,
Read the signs, watch and learn.

Still Alive!

As I awake at the start of day
I clasp my hands as if to pray,
But before I start I spread them out,
Stretch my arms and give a shout.

The sheets I'm in are not a shroud
I'm still in bed, not on a cloud,
I'm 82 and feeling good
And I thank the lord – 'there ain't no wood!'

That Brumijum One, Two, Three

I'd like to be the speaking clock
With people calling me,
They'd lift their phone
At work or home
And dial that one, two, three.

But I can see a problem
When I answer to their call,
My voice, you see,
It's really me,
I'm a Brummie to the core.

Being born and bred a Brummie
Some folks won't understand,
It's the voice they'll hear
So coarse on ear,
Can sometimes get out of hand.

So I've settled on a solution
And it's one that's not been tried,
The folks I'd use
Are those who choose
To live in Brum from far and wide.

Twelve noon 'till two could be Arabic
And two 'till four, Japanese,
With most of the rest,
That's right, you've guessed,
Would be all types of Brumijese.

Six 'till eight could be Hindu
With eight 'till ten in Welsh,
The ten 'till twelve's
Could please themselves
'Cos I'd be somewhere else!

Every day could be so different,
Many cultures with some in rhyme,
All would get
No more, no less,
Than their accurate allotted time.

Part of this could be time off
For holidays and special needs,
We could break at seven
'Till going on eleven
Just to have our cup of tea.

There'd be training times for all involved
Bond building would make us friendly,
Creating this team
Might well be a dream
But a nightmare seems more likely!

Can you now begin to imagine
When folks dial those one, two, threes,
Back down the phone
In that Brumijum tone,
'Dyownow wa toim it is?'

'Tek ya finga orf dem buttins,
Gi us arffamo, awroit,
If yow wan the toim
It's affpass noin,
Tha's terday an no'ternoight!'

'Oil tellya wor toim it is
If yowl shutya gob, awroit,
Now ang a sec,
O blinkin 'ec,
No oim gonna avta do it twoice!'

Maybe now you see the reason
Why this scene could never be,
I doubt, with a smile,
That folks would dial
That Brumijum one, two, three!

The Chair under the Stairs

There's a place when I'm low
Where I can just go,
To relax, unwind or chill.
It has an old oak chair,
In the hall, under stairs,
At a house on top of a hill.

The views from the grounds
Reach for miles around,
Covering mountains, a castle and sea.
But the thing I like best,
Is being able to rest,
In the chair, under stairs, and just me.

Its space has no door
Just three walls and a floor,
With a ceiling under the stairs.
There's a small window for light,
For me to read, rest or write,
Sat down in this old oak chair.

Ground views, there are none,
That's part of the fun,
Time to gaze at pictures on walls.
Sat down in that chair,
Under the stairs,
Relaxed, no stresses at all.

With dawn's early light
Easing darkness to bright,
The chair claims a hue of its own.
Its old oak frame,
Shows no sign of a strain,
As I sit on this worn seated throne.

Its age I would guess,
One hundred at least,
Leaving a thought that enters my mind.
How many others,
Have taken the bother,
To enjoy its peace that I find?

Over long time,
Oak ages like wine,
Growing stronger and deeper in tone.
But chairs comfort remains,
Easing all of my pains,
From mental and physical zones.

Today's place for the chair,
Is under the stairs,
In the hall of a house on a hill.
Old oak it may be,
But it's a comfort to me,
Tomorrow, I hope it's there still!

The Dancing Seagull

Casually walking down a seaside street,
I spotted a seagull stamping his feet.
Totally amazed at this unusual sight,
I crept up easy, not wishing to fright.

There he was, grey feathers and all,
Warming his feet, having a ball.
He'd stop now and then to take a quick peak,
Scratching the grass with the tip of his beak.

I looked all about, tried catching the sound,
That started him dancing and stamping the ground.
No music I heard to set him off prancing,
And he'd start off again right after his beaking.

By now a large crowd had gathered to meet,
This strange little bird with the delicate feet.
There he was with his peaking and prancing,
That little seagull with his two feet dancing.

A thought crossed my mind, I knew it made sense,
By taking a whipround I could make a few pence.
So off with my hat and quietly I asked,
'Spare a few bob for this incredible task.'

Some were obliging, others quite rude,
'Don't you see that bird is dancing for food?'
The thought had occurred, no doubt about that,
But those that gave, quickly filled up my hat.

But then a large cat appeared on the scene,
Frightfully big and awfully mean.
With one mighty pounce, had that bird in its jaw,
The crowd moved off and the bird was no more.

Many worms now appeared with their heads above ground,
Looking about, pinpointing that sound.
That steady thumping had brought them to light,
But now they'd arrived, no bird was in sight.

Two boys then arrived all covered in muck,
One spotted the worms and shouted 'jus' look.'
'There's worms right here on top of the ground,'
The other one said 'that's sound, real sound.'

They collected those worms, near filling a tin,
Then wandered off carrying two poles with a pin.
'Going fishing' they said, 'not far from here,
Down on the jetty or under the pier.'

That bird had provided, bait for those two,
Had amused a crowd with something to view,
I'd made a bob by passing my hat,
But that poor dancing bird lost out to the cat.

The Day before Christmas

It was the day before Christmas,
No spare till in sight,
Those queues, never ending,
Stress starting to bite.

Loaded down with a turkey,
Spuds, carrots and sprouts,
I've been standing for hours
Just trying to get out.

Outside, light has faded,
Cold winds start to blow,
It seems miles to the car park
And it's starting to snow.

'This year is the last one,'
A queueing neighbour retorts,
'Next year we're away
To some Spanish resort!'

'It won't be the same,'
I heard myself say,
'Not being at home
To enjoy Christmas Day.

You know how you'd miss it,
Friends 'round for tea,'
But those words just uttered,
Sparked an envy in me.

I'm worn out, collapsing,
And my feet are red hot,
Just why am I queueing
When my family is not?

Each Christmas, a fortune,
Kids demanding the best,
You please one or two
And upset all the rest.

The wrapping and hiding,
'Father Christmas won't come,'
A threat for the youngsters,
But not the grown ones.

'No such bloke, Father Christmas,
It's a neighbour or you,'
Getting older means smarter,
Bone idle too!

Each till now is flat out,
A small fortune they're taking,
I'm weighed down with essentials,
Every muscle now aching.

'That's it, enough,
Get out of my way,
I'm postponing our Christmas
To a less hectic day!'

Limping away from my trolley,
I turned around, left the queue,
When two security persons
Then hove into view.

One said quite firmly,
'You can't leave that there,'
Folks all around
Began starting to stare.

'It's company policy,'
The other one said,
'You can't abandon a trolley
With a turkey that's dead!'

This to me, was like,
Red rag to a bull,
With blood pressure rising,
To the point of, 'near full'.

'When I started queueing,
That bird was alive,
It was a week last Tuesday
At a quarter past five!'

'Now, now,' they both echoed,
'There's no need for that,
If it ain't going with you
You'd best put it back.

These queues are for buying,
Not leaving trolleys about,
If you're going to be awkward,
We'll escort you out!'

I heard then much grumbling,
Folks starting to moan,
Trolleys being abandoned,
Many heading for home.

'You're right, I'm off,
It's wasting my time,
I'm off down the pub
For nibbles and wine.'

'I'll phone an old aunty,
I ain't seen in years,
Get invited for Christmas,
Just take a few beers!'

'The pressies are sorted,
Find a hotel, down south,
Any food I've not cooked
Will taste sweet in my mouth!'

These comments came flying,
From all over the place,
Those security persons
Had alarm on their face.

By now, queues were stampeding,
With folks rushing for cars,
All leaving their trolleys
Just where they are.

The raw edge I'd hit on,
Had sparked everyone off,
Leaving queues almost empty
But for trolleys with stuff.

The two security persons,
Then called out for more,
Summoning others to clear up,
The trolley bogged floor.

Cool as a cucumber,
I returned to my place,
Quietly pushing my trolley
With ever quickening pace.

I paid for my goods,
But before I cleared off,
Caught the ear of who served me,
With a discreet gentle cough.

'It works every time,
When the queue is severe,
Merry Christmas to you
And a Happy New year!'

The Face at the Window

There's a face at the window
In a house down the street,
With eyes that miss nothing
Much higher than feet.

All day it stares out
Catching the wind stir the leaves,
Rarely much higher
Than those feet to the knees.

Passing folks seldom notice
This all day glare,
Watching anything moving
With its permanent stare.

It's been there forever
Least that's how it seems,
With a head full of black hair
And its world full of dreams.

The face whiskers need trimming
But there's no hint of a beard,
On the face that just watches
Never saying a word.

It watches birds with their feeding
Teaching young ones to fly,
But it's things at ground level
That catches its eye.

It spots a mouse or a mole
That you and I miss,
With a stare once settled,
Never moves, not a twitch.

It rearranges the curtains
To better its view,
Missing nothing that's moving
Like the odd neighbour or two.

There's the pair from the new house
With identical twins,
Who pause at the gateway,
The face catches their grins.

There's that miserable old gent
From three doors below,
Who cusses the face,
Shakes his fist but then goes.

There's the kids from the school bus
That stops right outside,
Some will shout and call names,
But the face stays inside.

There's the bread and the post
And the coalman too,
All pause for a chat
When the face is on view.

Some bring food to the face
With a comfort or two,
The face shows its pleasure
As all receiving should do.

But it's night-time it likes
As the best time of all,
Sneaking out with the dark
Through the door down the hall.

Still keeping its face
A few inches from ground,
What it misses to see,
It catches with sound.

Each night 'face' is out
'Till dawn's morning light,
Coming home with the milkman,
Now that is a sight.

Then the face just sleeps
'Till its dinner is due,
Then it's back to the window,
As most cats do!

The Future Snowman

Two sisters will be building a snowman
In their garden a few years from now.
As the snow gets thicker
The sisters get quicker,
Spurred on by the fresh falling snow.

The older will be rolling the tummy,
The younger, the arms and the head.
By rolling it around
Where there's grass to be found,
Each piece will grow from the size of an egg.

Three pieces will be used for the body
By stacking them end on end.
A good scrape down
From top to the ground
And a shape will be starting to blend.

Next will come a stick through the shoulders
Then arms can be fixed to the sides.
On goes the head,
With a nose carrot red,
And a hat that will be starting to slide.

Small stones will form buttoned jacket,
Two tomatoes, rosy red cheeks.
His two green eyes
Will be a cucumber sliced,
Bits of coal, his eyebrows and teeth.

Mom's scarf will drape around his neck,
Old gloves will form his hands.
And just for good taste
Around his waist,
Dad's belt will form a band.

Last comes the delicate sculpting
And legs begin to appear.
Using a small child's spade ,
A cut will be made,
'Till a gap will be seen quite clear.

Then future snowmen will be finished
And we invited to peek.
'Take a look grandma,'
'Come and see grandpa,'
And Christmas will be complete.

The Parrot and the Plum

A parrot woke up one morning
In a state of some distress.
He found a plum,
Had been glued to his bum,
And his feathers in an awful mess.

The parrot quickly decided
'There is no time to lose.
I'll ask a chum,
To remove this plum,
Or even eat it if they choose.'

The parrot started walking,
Determined a friend to find.
His heartfelt plea,
Was heard by a flea,
'Oh would you be so kind,'

'I've a plum on my bum'
Said the parrot to the flea,
'It's making a mess
Of my feathered dress,
Do you fancy some for tea?'

The flea said to the parrot,
'I don't know why you're asking me.
I only dine,
On friends feline,
That's my usual place for tea.'

The parrot walked on downhearted,
Now feeling quite absurd,
When he saw two wings
And heard it sing,
'I think I'll ask that bird.'

'I've a plum on my bum'
Said the parrot to the bird.
'To have one there
Is extremely rare,
And it makes me look absurd'

The bird said to the parrot
'You really look a mess,
I'm too small
To eat it all,
Try the fish at this address.'

To have a fish come recommended
Might be just the friend he'd need,
So off he went,
With good intent,
To remove that plum with speed.

'I've a plum on my bum'
Said the parrot to the fish.
'It won't go away,
It's here to stay,
And to remove it is my wish.'

The fish said to the parrot
'I can only swim around.
I've just these fins
For moving things,
Have a word with next door's hound.'

The parrot kept on walking,
Soon found the house next door,
But what he found
Was not one hound,
It was a pack of twenty-four!

The parrot by now was shaking,
Those hounds a fearsome sight.
Fish, birds and fleas,
He'd met with ease,
But those hounds gave him a fright!

'I've a plum on my bum' said the parrot,
His voice already trembling,
'So I'll just run
And take my plum,
To a friend outside who's waiting.'

The parrot ran as fast as he could,
Out of the gate and into the wood.
As he ran, he coughed
And the plum fell off
Straight onto a goose!

The parrot was delighted,
The goose said shocked and bemused,
'I'll ask a chum
To remove this plum,
Or even eat it if they choose!'

The Passing of Bert

A cry rang out from the upper deck,
'Has anyone seen my Bert?
He's a small thin chap
With a tartan cap,
Matching shorts and lime green shirt.

His socks are blue but not so new,
A little thin at the heels and toes.
I made him change his pants
As we left France
And they're red with two small holes.

The shades he wears cause folks to stare,
Pink frames without the lenses,
But I think he's class
Without the glass
And his squinting rocks my senses.

I sat him there in my deck chair
And told him not to move,
But he gets head strong
If I'm gone too long
And does just what he'd choose.

For thirty years I've bent his ears,
Convinced I know what's right,
But if I'm not there
He trogs off anywhere,
To mix with folks that I won't like.

It's me who gets him up each day
And decides just what we'll do.
I choose his clothes
'Cos heaven knows,
He'd rather wear a suit.'

Bert's wife out loud had drawn a crowd,
To ponder her commotion.
Four crewmen came
Then left again,
No English and no notion.

Then the Captain came and took the strain,
Organising all around.
'Don't panic ma'am,
Just stay calm,
I'm sure he'll soon be found.'

The boat was stopped and the anchor dropped,
Then searched from stern to stem.
They did it twice,
Which Bert's wife thought nice,
But no sign of Bert, he'd gone.

'I just know he's in and my Bert can't swim,
Not one stroke without his duck.
My Bert has drowned
And can't be found,
What a dreadful piece of luck.'

Then came a cry from quite close by,
'lime green on the starboard bow.
I'm sure it's Bert,
Or at least his shirt,
His wife is bound to know.'

The Captain said 'If it's Bert he's dead,
The way he's floating in the sea.
Send out a boat
With a grappling rope
And drag him back to me.'

The boat came back with a plastic sack,
Sealed tight and full of air.
Around one side,
Someone had tied,
A shirt like Bert would wear.

On the other side a small chap could ride,
In two stirrups of old blue socks.
'They belong to Bert,
I'd know his shirt,
As well as I know my frocks.'

With a Captain's charm, he took her arm,
'I'm afraid your Bert is lost,
But don't you mind
I'm sure you'll find,
The company will bear the cost.

From this very day there's no more to pay,
All cruises for you are free.
Your Bert's just drowned
And can't be found
On that we all agree.'

The boat carried on into the sun,
Bert's passing soon forgotten,
But below the deck
And soaking wet,
Stood Bert in shorts of tartan.

'I was about all in when you dragged me in,
Me and my tartan shorts,
But I'm not going home
To hear her moan,
No way I'm getting caught.'

The crew agreed and with due speed,
Hid Bert until they docked.
In borrowed clothes
He hit the road,
His future now unlocked.

Bert's unwidowed wife found a brand new life,
Cruising with the Captain.
Of Bert, it's known
He's prone to roam,
But not on water, that's for certain!

The Usual

I just want an old fashioned barber,
One who cuts hair and shaves.
I have no need
For a coiffeur degree,
Just one who knows me and my ways.

I like a chat to pass the time,
While my remnant hair is trimmed.
I enjoy life's jokes
One shares with blokes,
And the feel of a 'cut throat' on skin.

I don't have the hair for highlights,
Or those bits at the back, grade two.
The long strands that remain,
Cover my scalp in the rain,
And my greyness will just have to do.

It may not appear that important,
Just a whim on my part, sheer pride.
But the hair that I've got,
Has ceased growing on top,
So I comb it from side to side.

I'll wash my hair in the sink at home,
Let the bits blow away with the breeze.
I'll have no cologne,
Or grease like foam,
Just a trim and a shave if you please!

But hairdressers are not like barbers,
They need to feel and weigh it all up.
I've no time for that,
There's more hair on our cat,
And the bit that I've got ain't a mop.

Hairdressers are stylists they'd have you believe,
Trained to cut each hair to perfection.
But, they do need hair,
And if there ain't much there,
A barber's the simplest solution.

I can't be doing with all that perusing,
Counting my few bits of hair.
I'm into the seat,
Then out tidy and neat,
In five minutes flat, no more.

So, 'the usual sir,' is all that I need,
My barber can trim without fear.
A scrape 'round my face,
And each strand put in place,
Layered over from ear to ear!

Thinks

Said Mrs Think to Mr Think,
'Ivor, I think I have need of a child.
If it's O.K. with you,
'Could be the start of a few,
Will you think on it, just for a while?'

Said Mr Think to Mrs Think,
'Ursula, I think I will think on that.
Some Thinks extra
Does sound better,
I think I'll put on my thinking cap.'

Said Mrs Think to Mr Think,
'Think, I think you may need to rush.
I'm going to town
For a maternity gown,
I'm thinking I'd best catch the bus.'

Now Think got down to his thinking,
About those things Mrs Think had just said.
'Going to town,
And maternity gown,'
Think had thoughts, thinking things, in his head.

'Am I thinking of Thinks of the future,
Or am I thinking it's about to be?
When Ursula gets back,
I think I'll ask her just that,
'Cos I'm thinking we Thinks could be three.'

After a while Think turned to a smile,
'Another Think? I think I could manage the one!'
Then the phone bell called
And his Ursula bawled,
'Think, quit your thinking and come.

I was 'round at your mother's when nature took over
And now we're not two Thinks but three.
That bump on my front,
You thought was the mumps,
Was an extra Think about to be free.'

Think ran straight out and started to shout,
'I'm a father now there's a new Think like me.'
Then on quick to his mom's,
Where he had begun,
And a wee Think had now come to be.

As Thinks settled down, Ivor put it around,
In effect, that he was the planner.
But it's obvious when,
Once written in pen,
I think,
U think,
And wee Think,
Sounds right, and good English grammar!

Thongs for the Memory

My thong's gone wrong, it's looking sad,
I'm sure my bum ain't meant to sag.
If it does and folks can see,
Does it stretch below my knee?

Old type pants covered all my bum,
But thongs are sparse and a lot more fun.
Not much cover should I ever fall,
Where oh where do I tuck it all?

Could lift a little or try lose a lot,
Maybe draw it in and tie a knot.
I walk around with tautened cheeks,
But my bum goes numb within a week.

When winter comes I feel the draught,
But wear two pairs? Now that's a laugh.
I'd rather freeze and keep my pride
Than wear a pair on either side.

They're just a fashion, a current trend,
Something you'd only show a friend,
Not meant to cover or keep you warm,
And there ain't enough to mend, if torn.

So, for the moment, I'll keep mine on,
Until the fashion has been and gone.
Then back to pants, or better still,
Forget them all and wear a kilt!

Three's a Crowd

'What shall we do on holiday daddy,
What shall we do by the sea,
What shall we do in the day daddy,
What shall we do after tea?

Will there be sand I can dig daddy,
Will there be games I can play,
Will there be ice cream and pop daddy,
Will the sun really shine every day?

Can I join in with the kids daddy,
Can I spend all day in the pool,
Can I have a ride on a donkey daddy,
Can you be sure I'm not going to fall?

Are we going to go to the fair daddy,
Are we going to run on the sand,
Are we going to get up early daddy,
Are you going to let go of my hand?

Is there time to spare for it all daddy,
Is there enough light in the day,
Is there too much I'm wanting to do daddy,
Is there enough in your pocket to pay?

Have I addled your brain daddy,
Have I scrambled the thoughts in your head,
Have I harped on now for a bit daddy,
Have you heard a word that I've said?'

*

'Come sit here awhile and I'll tell you my child,
Of wonderful things yet to be.
During the day we'll stay out the way,
Sharing a towel on a beach by the sea.

At the start of our day I'll lie watching you play,
With styrene and bottles you'll find.
I'll repair an old spade for to dig in the shade,
And our rubbish you'll bury behind.

Then just before noon, not a moment too soon,
I'll be away down the pub.
You, my child, will snooze for a while,
In a cool spot you'll dig in the mud.

With my pubbing all done you'll be ready for fun,
But I'll be in need of a nap.
You'll just have to shush, try making no fuss,
No ice cream or pop, just the tap.

With my snoozing complete you'll be up on your feet,
But the headache I'll have won't allow.
You'll play on the rocks in your old shoes and socks,
And I'll catch up later, somehow.

Once we're together there'll be a turn in the weather,
Some rain, even hail or snow.
The tide will rush in, too cold for a swim,
Back to our tent then is where we will go.

Once we get there, if there's some time to spare,
I'll teach you to gamble for cash.
In no time at all I'll have taken it all,
And be back down the pub in a flash.

While I'm away it's okay to play,
With the kids from the posh hotel.
If you're invited for tea, save some for me,
I'll be hungry and feeling unwell.

The only donkeys you'll see are those that we need,
Down the cliff path from campsite to beach.
You can't have a ride, they'll be much too tired,
Carrying the towel and tan oil I'll need.

As for running on sand, I won't be holding your hand,
My beer belly won't allow for such fun.
Run if you will to the top of the hill,
I'll have a smoke in the time you'll be gone.

Come now my child, where gone has your smile,
Wipe your nose and try not to cry.
It's on holiday we're going and disappointment is showing,
I can't begin to imagine just why!'

*

'Oh husband of mine, you do spin a line,
Styrene and bottles indeed.
There's no tent and no mud, nor all day in the pub,
The hotel has catered our needs.

The sands are fantastic, no sign of your plastic,
You won't have to mend an old spade.
With a pool chair for each, set close to the beach,
No shared towel for one in the shade.

There's plenty to do for our child and you,
So we can all relax and just chill.
Without any cliffs your path won't exist,
Just a beach from the sea to the hills.

It's no wonder our child has forgotten to smile,
With cheeks that are wet from her tears.
Aggravation's not fun when it goes on and on,
You keep forgetting her tender young years.

It's time you behaved, started changing your ways,
Try to see what a darling she is.
She stands tall in a crowd and you should be proud,
She's your daughter, our sweet little miss.'

*

Sweet little miss, sweet little miss,
Have you heard the whine of that girl?
She stands tall in a crowd 'cos her voice is so loud,
And I seem to cop for it all.

I know who she is and I love her to bits,
But on holiday I need to relax.
You both spend all year, bending my ear,
I'm exhausted and that is a fact.

So I exaggerate a bit, but most times it fits,
It's far better than losing my cool.
If the truth is known, we should have come on our own,
But they won't have our girl back at school.'

*

'Now that is enough you two, I'm off,
It's always the same when we come.
If dad's not complaining, the weather is raining,
Why can't we all just get on and have fun?

I don't mind sarcastic and I'm good with my plastic,
And wet sand's the best place to dig.
The last donkey I sat, got collapsed, squashed and flat,
'Cos I used to be small now I'm big.

I'm no longer a child with a heart softening smile,
I'm knocking on past thirty-two.
It's time I was off to do my own stuff,
Somewhere jet setting will do.

So next time you're looking at a holiday booking,
Count me out, I'll be off with a friend.
You two stay right here, I'm away for a beer,
Dad, the keys if you please, it's the car I'm going to lend.'

*

'Right Ma, has she gone, now we can have fun,
I never thought she'd go for the hint.
She's gone thirty-two, grown up through and through,
Our life from now on should be MINT'!

To School on a Bus

As a small lad I went to school on a bus,
With homework late and a mother's fuss.
Two thrupenny bits, my total fares,
One hour it took just to get me there.

Short trousers and blazer, regulation attire,
Trousers ever shorter as I grew higher.
Week long socks way below my knees,
Back of legs chapped by a cold winter breeze.

Satchel so heavy on my shoulders so small,
With bits tied on to carry it all.
No-one ever offered to share my load,
As I bussed each day on my long school road.

Giving up my seat to a lady in need,
Considered polite, not just a good deed.
Move down the aisle 'till up with the driver,
Watch changing gears, I could do it, no bother.

Loosen the satchel, homework to be checked,
Sneak a banana, repack the rest.
Forgot the pumps tied on at the end,
Missed out on P.E., so tried that again.

In earlier days never ventured up top,
That was for smokers, I could tell by the cough.
But the best place of all was right by the bell,
To give it a tweak when no-one could tell

Brakes would jam on and bus skid to a stop,
Mass choking would start for smokers on top.
Old folks collapsed down the aisle with a bang,
Each looking at others to see who it was rang.

Driver came 'round to sort out the mess,
Red in the face with so much stress.
Conductor would glower in my direction,
But angelic boy looks denied implication.

Return journeys were hectic as queues gathered face,
All jostling with others to achieve the right place.
Buses arrive full to the top,
Chains across platforms, no intention to stop.

'No pushing, no shoving,' conductor would bawl,
'Room for one only,' or 'no room at all.'
Satchels were loosened to fall to the ground,
While victims were searching, others ran 'round.

'Standing room only' he would call with a roar,
'Move right inside, make room for one more.'
Those that got on, all packed like sardines,
No matter how tight, all wearing broad grins.

To ride on the platform on a hot summer's day,
That breeze, a pleasure, for whatever you'd pay.
But on cold winter days, right down inside,
The engine up front made a warm place to ride.

As those journeys went on and nearing my stop,
Make my way to the platform, ready for off.
To alight before stopping, so risky, a dare,
To jump and then run as if floating on air.

Then trudge on home, school work to be done,
Before 'playing out', before having fun.
Swing open the door never needing a key,
'I'm home our mom, what's to eat, what's for tea?'

True Brit

The Germans have woken, poolside has been taken,
And its only just coming to dawn.
There's towels, bath robes and most of their clothes,
Will pool war break out once its warm?

The Belgians arrive, most choosing to hide,
Recalling what's gone on before.
Quietly shuffling around, not making a sound,
Staying neutral, this time, if it's war.

Italian ladies parade, both in sunshine and shade,
True elegance for all to admire.
Then grandmothers appear, all in black, and oh dear,
Years of pasta producing spare tyres.

The Austrians too, stand politely to queue,
Not wishing to appear out of place.
There's a tolerance here, developed in years,
With a firmness etched deep in the face.

Then the Spaniards come to soak up the sun,
Clicking fingers and calling 'ole'.
Once settled, no move, as if stuck down with glue,
No more working as waiters today.

Portuguese, there are few, maybe one, sometimes two,
Trying hard to blend with the rest.
The strange words that they use, leave others confused,
But their English, superb, at its best.

Then out comes the sun, Brits line up for fun,
Trepidation now filling the air.
Once lager starts flowing, all there will be knowing,
Brits rarely, if ever, play fair.

'Good morning my dears, may I welcome you here,'
The maitre D asks all, but aloud.
'It will be nice at the pool with sunbed and stool,
Our sky is pure blue, not a cloud.'

'Do we stand out as rubbish, can they tell who is British?'
There's always one fool that inquires.
'Don't we look as smooth, real sharp, in a groove,
Do our socks need to go even higher?'

'It's that shellsuit and you Sir, that gave us a clue Sir,
The same one's been worn here for years.
And one has just noticed, the band aid and poultice,
On that boil at the back of your ear.'

'Nice one my man, now this is the plan,
Those Germans will just have to stroll.
We can't have a game, those sun beds, a pain,
We need goals at both ends of the pool.'

Faced with unsubtle persuasion of shouting and waving,
Those in the pool soon got out.
Sunbeds relocated, The poolside vacated,
'Us Brits v. The Rest', came the shout.

The few Portuguese would have nothing of this,
The Belgians had quietly sloped off.
The Austrians too, had taken dim view,
And the Spaniards cried off with a cough

The Italians, to a man, ushered ladies and gran,
Away from this battle they saw.
Leaving just Germans and Brits, with a score yet to fix,
Would this be the outbreak of war?

The Germans dived in, the Brits couldn't swim,
So they entered the pool down the steps.
With 'true Brit', as it were, they avoided the glares,
'Till pool water reached a hair on their chests.

With the water quite cool, don't squeal, act the fool,
But don't let those Germans catch on.
With much lager inside and nowhere to hide,
Just pee in the pool 'till its gone.

They let the contest commence, all knew it made sense,
With footy on the telly at three.
As the battle was locked, all at poolside got soaked,
But neither side gave an inch, you could see.

After an hour, a Brit called 'Hey flower
Just what sort of game have we here?'
A German replied, with a look more than snide
'Vater polo of course, mein jung Herr.'

'Oh no it's not,' came the voice of a toff,
Located right there, by the pool.
'From where one is sitting, it's more boring than knitting,
There's little passion, no fighting, just fools.'

Both sides then surrendered, no score had been entered,
No record of fouls or sent off.
The pool quickly emptied, united passion was vented,
On the mouthpiece who spoke like a toff.

As he and sunbed were gathered, he became a mite lathered,
True fear now beginning to show.
He entered the pool, with both sunbed and stool,
As far as two Germans could throw.

The Brits all applauded, the Germans ignored it,
'It vas sumsing ve just 'ad to do.'
Off they all trogged to watch the match on the box,
'Back tomorrow, old son, here at two.'

Turkey Thoughts

A turkey strutting in the yard, thought,
It's not much fun is this,
We get taken out for Christmas,
But it's New Years Eve we miss.

They stuff us up with extra corn
So we can barely hobble,
Then load us up in one big truck,
With hardly room to gobble.

The journey could last for minutes or days,
We've just no way of knowing,
No-one ever comes back here,
To tell us where we're going.

It seems a little strange to me,
The fact that none return,
Where do they all spend New Year's Eve,
Haven't we a right to learn.

Why do we always spend our Christmas,
Away from our domestic scene,
Do they throw us all a party,
In this place where we've not been.

I believe the Caribbean,
Is warm this time of year,
I've seen it in the papers,
Blowing through the yard 'round here.

And then again the Cote d'Azure,
Sees sunshine all year through,
Sunny Spain for New Year's Eve,
Any one of these would do.

Beyond New Year there's Easter,
I'm told then turkeys go a bomb,
Perhaps that's where we're heading,
In this truck we're getting on.

Mind the feathers my good driver man,
They take a while to grow,
And I've a need to look pristine,
Not ruffled, I'll have you know.

Right, are we all on board and cosy,
Eh up, I think we're moving off,
I heard the engine starting,
As the driver gave a cough.

I don't think there's call to panic,
Now the driver's started singing,
We'll all join in the chorus,
So folks will know we're coming.'

'It's a long way, to tip a turkey,
It's a long way, to go.
It's a long way, to tip a turkey,
For the sweetest meat I know.

Goodbye, to Piccadilly,
Farewell Leicester Square.
It's a long, long way to tip a turkey,
But we're going, so there!'

Unibikey

I met a chap on a unicycle riding down the prom,
And paused to ask,
About his task,
'Why not two wheels, instead of one?'

The bikey then came to a stop, balancing on his wheel,
His face, quite calm,
As he took my arm,
'I'll let you know the deal.

Down the lanes, became a pain, too narrow for a trike,
Most cars, so fast,
As they drove past,
A situation I did not like.

I changed then to a tandem but a 'stoker', hard to find,
And it all felt wrong,
On a bike so long,
With no companion perched behind.

I opted then for two wheels and a multitude of gears,
Hills proved hard to climb,
On a ring of forty-nine.
And down, too fast on a twenty-three.

Then I came upon a unicycle with fixed gear and single wheel,
Now speed's my own,
Wherever I roam,
And uphill ain't no big deal.

Downhill I peddle backwards, uphill I'm off and walk,
I lean on my bike,
Wherever I like,
If someone asks, I stop and talk.

But one thing that I have noticed, an advantage on the rest,
On a one-wheel bike,
I stand just where I like,
And going backwards is the best.

Now I can hear you thinking, why on earth would I do that,
With some signs so long,
I get them wrong,
If I read and rush straight past.

I back up and start all over, without having to dismount,
Taking my time,
In a true straight line,
Making each separate letter count.'

This statement had me puzzled, I know nowhere like that,
Each sign I know,
Reads in one go,
Fairly short, and that's a fact.

'Before you go, I have to know, where is this sign you've seen,
Have you got it wrong,
No signs so long,
Where is this place you've been?'

The bikey started grinning, from his pack he drew a map,
It unfolded neat,
And on a seat,
He squatted down, I sat.

He pointed to an isle he knew, just off the coast of Wales,
'Anglesey' he said,
As he turned his head,
'On there, the legend of this tale'.

So, one nice day, if you're out that way, don't consult the clock,
You can read it fine,
If you take your time,
It's – LLANFAIRPWLLGWYNGYLLGOGERYCHWYRNDROBWLLLLANTYSILIOGOGOGOCH!

Uppity Downy

Uppity downy, a large spider of note,
Coughed just the once, to clear his throat.
The web he was on, shot back like a sling,
Throwing Uppity forward, as if on a swing.

Straight on he shot, leaving home web behind,
The cough force created, snapped his web safety line.
Uppity went tumbling, flying through air,
Parted from home, removed from his lair.

Stunned by the movement, shocked by it all,
Uppity flew on, avoiding the wall.
Rolled up tight to protect his eight feet,
Shot out through the door, into the street.

Bounced up by a bus, hurled high in the air,
Uppity then landed in some old gents hair.
The hair wasn't thick, in fact it was thin,
Hair that was silver, not covering much skin.

Uppity clung on, like a limpet on stone,
Looked all about, no sign of his home.
The old gent didn't notice this addition to hair,
Once settled in, Uppity felt cosy in there.

It was warm, it was slippy, in need of some work,
But Uppity was a grafter, not one to shirk.
Once his bruising subsided, Uppity began,
Making new web so fast, his eight feet just ran.

Around both ears, small webs he made,
These used as anchors, somewhere in the shade.
When up to the task, covering bald spot began,
Uppity had vision, Uppity, a plan.

Day after day, Uppity would cross,
From one ear to the other, covering hair loss.
Until finally, the old gent, had no bald spot at all,
Uppity had finished, his fine web covered all.

Uppity believed, the old gent would approve,
With web covered hair, no way it would move.
No need for a comb, no need for a brush,
But Uppity forgot, the old gent might wash!

Early one morning, the old gent arose,
Slipped out of his bed, took off his night clothes.
Into the bathroom, turned on the tap,
Looked into the mirror, and removed his night cap.

The old gent caught sight, of large spider and web,
Collapsed to the floor, the shock struck him dead.
The neighbours first missed him, when water came through,
Laid out in the bathroom, unable to move.

'Look at his hair,' one of them said,
'It's covered in cobweb, how long's he been dead?'
'Not more than an hour, how can that be?'
'No spider is that fast, not one that I've seen!'

Uppity scarpered, before he was spotted,
'Cover another, no way, just forget it.
I'll do no more favours,' Uppity mused,
'I'm feeling neglected, upset and confused.'

By a pure stroke of luck, a passing stray cat,
Saw Uppity walking, thought, 'I'll have some of that.'
Flicked out a paw, placing Uppity on top,
Racing home fast, not wanting to stop.

Stray cat took him in, put Uppity to work,
Making fine webs, in the dust, and the dirt.
Catching flies, gnats, and unwanted fleas,
That drove stray cat mad, whenever they'd please.

Today, Uppity Downy is a spider relaxed,
Happy with life, pleased with his task.
But don't ask him to make, a web for your head,
The last one he made, left some old gent quite dead!

Various Veins

'It's various veins'
Doc's reception explained,
'It's various veins of the leg.
If you don't have them out,
It could lead to gout,
So I've booked you one hospital bed'.

Off I went on the bus,
Silk pyjamas, tooth brush,
Prepared to suffer all pain.
'I'm here with my veins,
It's all been arranged,
If you're busy, I'll call back again!'

'There's no need for that,
Lie down or be sat,
There's a queue over there you can join.'
So I hobbled on over
Using others for lever,
And caught some poor chap in the groin.

He collapsed in a heap
Right there at my feet,
With a vice-like grip on my veins.
I passed clean out,
Hit the floor with a clout,
Coming around to even more pain.

They put me to bed
Where my notes could be read,
By every Tom, Dick and Harry that passed.
'Various veins,' they all smirked,
'I'll bet that will hurt,
Best have the morphine, not just the gas!'

The ward cleaner just winced,
A young doctor advanced,
'It's various veins old son.
Still never you mind,
I'll just tuck them behind,
You won't see a thing when I'm done.'

I'm not one to complain
And can tolerate pain,
But to me this didn't seem right.
'You're having a laugh
And I've taken time off,
So I'm here on the ward for the night!'

'Well, as you insist,
You're now on my list,
I'll whip the things out after tea.
But don't come complaining
If the weather starts raining,
And you can't feel a thing from the knee!'

To me, the doc just seemed,
A mite less than keen,
And for the 'op', he just did his best,
But as I got home
The young doc's on the phone,
'It's about your post-op request.'

'I've cut open kings
For the smallest of things
But no-one ever asked me before.
You want to retain
The old part of your vein,
May I ask you, what on earth for?'

I merely replied
With loud audible sigh,
'As a lad my dad gave me one.
It dries out to elastic,
Much stronger than plastic,
And gives many hours of fun.

But two weeks ago,
The elastic let go,
And snapped in two in my hand.
I have need of another,
If it's not too much bother,
The one you've just snipped would be grand.'

From way down the phone,
All I heard was a groan,
Followed by a loud piercing yell.
'You're using a vein,
Time and again,
As elastic, don't ring my bell!'

'Doc, it's the truth,
And if you're looking for proof,
Next time try a vein of your own.
Right now I need one,
To play with my son,
Put mine in the post to my home!'

Next day it turned up,
Not by post, with the doc,
'I need to see just what it will do.'
So I fitted it in,
Gave propeller a spin,
Our model plane took off and just flew.

The doc staggered back,
Face all aghast,
'I've seen but still can't believe.
The strength in the vein,
Lasts time and again,
I see a fortune in those I retrieve.'

The last that I heard,
And good to his word,
The doc, his fortune had made.
He sells various veins
With his own brand name,
'Vein elastic', a whole new trade.

I'm living on,
All leg pain now gone,
With 'vein elastic' doing the 'bis'.
If only I'd seen
Before doc had his dream,
'Vein elastic' would be mine, not his!

Vera Lynn

'Half a pound of Vera Lynn,'
A little boy called from the back.
'Half a pound of Vera Lynn,
Me mam'll stew it for the cat.
Half a pound of Vera Lynn,
Make it nice and fresh.
Half a pound of Vera Lynn,
No fat, it makes a mess.'

'Just you wait my little mate,'
The butcher shouted back,
'I've plenty in of Vera Lynn,
It's in a freezer on a rack.
I'll be quick and serve these ladies,
They're all in front of you,
Then I'll slice the Lynn all nice and thin
For your mom at home to stew.'

I couldn't stand it any longer,
What on earth was Vera Lynn?
I'd heard about the singer
But it's a butchers shop I'm in.
Other folks were queuing
All waiting to be served,
And this little boy's persistence
Was getting on my nerves.

The little boy was shuffling,
Kicking a football 'round the floor,
Then came a crash of battered glass
As a big lass pushed the door.
That door, it flew wide open
And in stormed little boy's mom,
'Have you asked the man for Vera Lynn,
I've a cat to feed back home?'

'Mam, I've asked the man for half a pound,
He says I've got to wait,
There's all these ladies queuing here,
It's them that's made me late.
He knows our cat is hungry,
I've already told him that,
But Vera Lynn cut nice and thin
Is kept in fridges on a rack.'

To little boy's mom this wasn't on,
Her cat at home came first.
She jumped the queue, little boy in tow,
The butcher feared the worst.
'I'm sorry you're all queueing
But you'll just have to wait,
Our cat at home is hungry
And she's ferocious if I'm late.

Now listen here my butcher man,
It's Vera Lynn I need,
They'll have to wait, I daren't be late,
I've a cat back home to feed.'
The butcher took a deep breath
To full height of five foot four,
Came steaming round the counter,
And showed big lass the door.

'I'm sorry about your cat, I am,
But you're wrecking half my shop.
That's a pony for the damage,
Or else I'll call a cop.'
Big lass dug deep and began to weep,
'I only came for Vera Lynn.
There's your cash, but I'll be back,
I'll bring my cat straight in.'

Little boy in hand, big lass went,
And we began to relax,
But the butcher started shaking,
He knew that little boy's cat.
'I'm sorry all, we're closing,
Clear off now, sling your hook.'
But little boy's mum had beat him,
And the cat had the meanest look.

There it stood outside the door,
From nose to tail, nine foot four.
This was no cat that we all knew
But a full-grown tiger from a zoo.
'Half a pound of Vera Lynn,
Good butcher if you will,
Half a pound of Vera Lynn
And I'll try to keep her still.'

'Half a pound of Vera Lynn,
Madam it's a pleasure,
Half a pound of Vera Lynn,
Ain't your boy a little treasure.
I'll tell you what, take all I've got,
No charge, it's all on me,
Fourteen pounds, stewed to brown,
Should feed her for a week!'

' I told my boy you'd be a joy
To ask for Vera Lynn,
But do I have to bring the tiger
If I need to queue again?'
'It's hard to get is Vera Lynn,'
The butcher then replied,
'If I get some more, don't use the door,
Take her 'round the side.'

The tiger dragged the two back home
Weighed down with Vera Lynn,
Calmness then took over
To sooth the queue I'm in.
But curiosity killed the cat they say
And I'd just met a big one,
'Before I go, I need to know,
What an earth is Vera Lynn?'

The queue then started tittering,
Hiding mouths behind their hands.
I'd become to them, a stranger,
With their cockney rhyming slang.
All gathered close in front of me,
The butcher, he joined in,
'Whale meat again,' they chorused,
That's what they meant by Vera Lynn!'

Waiting Room Only

A posh lady in fur with a high pitched voice,
Could be heard by all, we had no choice,
'One is not used to waiting',
She was loud to proclaim,
'If one is not seen soon, one will go home again.'
Quick as a flash I was up off my jacksie,
Rushing outside to call her a taxi.

A chap at the front, a sickly fellow,
With bright red hair but skin all yellow,
Collapsed to his knees and began to wail,
'Not her again with the same old tale.
This room is for waiting by the sick and the skiving,
Not just for her with that high pitched whining.'

The reception lady in a purple skirt,
Clean white blouse and a look to hurt,
Reached through the slats where she could speak,
Grabbed the chaps ear and gave it a tweak.
'I'll have no more of this, your ranting and raving,
So, 'sit' you two and start behaving!'

Just then a small boy of two or three,
Said to his mom, 'I want to go wee,'
His mom with a voice that would have shattered butter,
Clenched her teeth and was heard to mutter,
'If you must, you must, but slide down from my knee,'
The little boy did and just went 'w-e-e-e-e'.

An elderly man of a hundred or more,
Shot in from the street to a round of applause.
His zimmer on wheels was attached to a hound,
And the old man called out, 'do you see what I've found.
He was tied to the butchers all covered in mud,
Now he's tied to my zimmer, he pulls me real good!'

A nice looking lass in mid to late teens,
With designer top and knee torn jeans,
Crossed to the slats but before she could talk,
Passed wind very loudly, folks started to walk.
'Sorry about that' came a voice so soft,
'It just seems to happen and it's worse if I cough!'

Sat next to me was a chap feeling down,
Fed up to the teeth with the largest of frowns.
I thought to enquire what had brought him so low,
He paused to tell me as he stood up to go.
'I keep getting the earache, it's the bane of my life,
So I'm here for a gag, not for me, for the wife!'

A couple in the corner, together it seems,
With hacking coughs and noses that streamed,
We're blaming each other for getting the flu,
'You gave it to me', 'no, I got it from you.'
By the time we get out, all will be wheezing,
All of us worse and most of us sneezing!

A schoolboy arrived from a school we all knew,
The room started smelling from the mess on his shoe.
'Get out' came the voice from behind those slats,
'And clean off that mess, try using some grass,'
The schoolboy replied with a cheeky shrug,
'I'll use a small stick 'cos I don't do drugs!

The doctor on duty had not meant to be heard,
With his door cracked open we could catch the odd word.
'Hound with a zimmer,' 'taxi' and 'smell',
Was reception complaining, how much would she tell?
Doc's answer to that was soon in the coming,
'That's it, enough, I'm off, I'm going!'

All this disruption appeared normal to me
But just at this point I awoke from my dream,
To find myself trapped in the dark and no phone,
The staff had locked up, missed me and gone home.
The cussing I used was beyond description,
I'd only called in for a repeat prescription!

Wild Child

I want to go wild,
Be a real wild child,
Splash about in puddles, in gutters.
Just hang about,
Be so chilled out,
Have my mates all total nutters.

Wheelie my bike,
No lights at night,
Dump it wherever I care.
Who needs brakes,
For goodness sake,
No way I'll be seen to be square.

Slurp when I like,
Burp, I just might,
Eat what I choose between meals.
No meals to a time,
Too close to my line,
Burgers and fries are the deal.

Wash when I need,
Never with speed,
Leave my clothes on a wet shower floor.
I-pod well on,
Same ear bending drum,
Ignore folks pounding the door.

Skate on my board,
'No way' warnings ignored,
Adopt a bad attitude air.
Cruise on the blades,
Always with shades,
Drive the oldies totally spare.

Bunk off from school,
Know it all, act the fool.
Teachers have nothing I need.
Some homework I'll do,
Just to get through,
Cribbed from a friend, the smart weed.

Always wear black,
Studs front and back,
Be a Goth, black make up and all.
Razor my jeans,
Pale skin to be seen,
Pierce lip, tongue and cheek, have a ball.

Start clubbing in teens,
Be the one to be seen,
Sharp threads my folks won't approve.
Designer labels I'll wear,
Well gel the hair,
Strut about in my own solid groove.

Just when it will be,
Will it happen for me,
Can I be the 'wild child' of my dreams?
I'm staying cool,
It's my first day at school,
And it's not as bad as it seems!

Winter Sno' Fun!

The winter's arrived
And your skin's turned blue,
It's never a cold
Always the flu.

Your joints are creaking
Through lack of sun,
The tan's long faded
And that cost a bomb.

Your shoes are soaked
With snow and then rain,
Those white lines appear
When they dry out again.

The clothes you're wearing
Are thin to the wind,
The ones you needed,
Last summer got binned.

The skin on your face
Feels like leather,
Don't blame the cream
It's only the weather.

The wind cracks your lips
'Till talking's a pain,
You doubt that you'll ever
Feel warm sun again.

Kids are out playing
Snowballing and sliding,
For grown-ups like you,
It's the mornings you're dreading.

You queue for the bus
When the car won't go,
It's only a frost
But it looks like snow.

Roads become ice rinks
With snow packed and polished,
The gritting's too late
With too few lorries.

Rain mixes with snow
Making dirty brown slush,
Everything is slipping,
No-one can rush.

Folks begin falling
Bruising their bones,
Hurting their pride,
They'd rather be home.

Snow falls at night,
Another foot by tomorrow,
You haven't a shovel
So buy one or borrow.

Neighbours come knocking,
Can you lend them a hand,
If you cleared their path
That would be grand.

Children are building
A den on your lawn,
Making blocks out of snow,
Inside should be warm.

By now you start thinking
How it was as a child,
You'd forgotten the fun,
You're missing the smiles.

So, on with the wellies,
Hat, jacket and scarf,
Dig out the sledge
And off to the park.

Tomorrow brings spring,
Today is for snow,
Just show those kids
They've a long way to go!

Yesterday's Chippie

Gone are the days
Of that faint blue haze
When fat was used for the frying.
Today they use oil
To come to the boil,
But it ain't the same as that dripping.

They used forefinger and thumb
To grip a fish by the bum
And drag every one thro' the batter.
To get each one right
'Till way late at night,
Was the 'art and sole' of the matter.

Not one chip was wasted
And none were ever tasted
Merely a squeeze was required.
We knew they were cooked
By the way that they looked,
Those folks with their lips lifting higher.

In those days gone by
Under a cold winter sky,
Fish and chips came wrapped in newspaper.
The vinegar soaked through
For the greedier few,
So hands stayed warm but stank later.

In the old days, no peas
Straight from a deep freeze,
They came boiled to a thick mushy state.
There was gravy too
For the hungrier few,
To take it all home, bring a plate.

In the old chippie shops
You could have the bits that came off,
As the fish and chips were in frying.
They were put to one side
Behind hot glass that would slide,
And were bought as a 'pen'orth of scratchings'.

Some old chippies sold pies
And they always smelt nice,
All steaming and hot in their pastry.
No matter what's inside
With chips on the side,
Made a nice change from fish with that gravy.

Some chip shops were caffs
Where you would meet for a laugh,
With mates or the one you were keen on.
There'd be a big bag of chips
And all took a 'dib',
Around that table no-one dared lean on.

In some of those shops
There'd be tables with cloths,
For those who could sit, eat and talk.
Most folks didn't care
There were only two chairs,
Three spoons, two knives and a fork.

The chip shops today
Have all changed in a way
We could never have known.
But one things the same
When it's your turn just say,
'Fish and chips, if you please, to take home.'

You and your Smile

If I could hold one thought of you,
The one that speaks to me of you,
I'd take the one I think of you,
That catches in your smile.

If I could hear the breath of you,
That wakes me as I lie with you,
I'd lie so still and look at you,
Just watching for your smile.

If I could repeat my time with you,
I'd put aside what saddened you,
And do again what pleasured you,
To one everlasting smile.

If I could take the pain from you,
That others seem to put on you,
I'd take it without complaint to you,
To help you keep that smile.

But then, I could imagine life with more of you,
If our children grow to be like you,
There'd be a lot more laughs with all of you,
And a thousand times the smiles!

You'll Know You're Old

You'll know you're old when you hate red wine,
Need to pee a few more times,
Cough so much your teeth fly out,
Don't bother with cups, drink from the spout.

You'll pass through a door and forget the way,
Won't always hear what others might say,
Can't read a paper except the headings,
Look for your name under births and weddings.

Still have a bike but spares are rare,
Comb your scalp instead of hair,
Walk with a limp from an old war wound,
But never saw service, you conniving hound.

The suit you'll wear will be old and shot,
Like state pension, it's all you've got,
'Bury me in it' is in your will,
The embalmers won't, it'll make them ill.

You'll use the park, walk on the grass,
'Gurn' your face at some wee lass,
She'll fetch the 'parky', they'll both complain,
You'll get banned but sneak back again.

The food you'll buy is 'get one free',
But who wants beans each day for tea,
You'd buy good booze but you're too tight,
You'll brew your own but it won't taste right.

You'll suck at a curry but no poppadoms,
The bits get trapped between plate and gums,
You liked it hot but now it's mild,
Your old insides should be fire clay tiled.

You'll use a sock to polish your shoes,
Won't wash clothes when they've been used,
Put food on the stove and watch the telly,
And only remember when the room turns smelly.

You'll have a wife and kids but all long gone,
They won't come around, they've escaped, moved on,
Your fall from grace will have been too much,
But you won't know that, you're in a rut.

If all of this sounds a little unreal,
Ask older folks, see how they feel,
Can they remember or have they heard,
Of course they won't, that's just absurd.

So take advice from one who knows,
Grab life now before it goes,
Old age will arrive in its own good time,
Enjoy what's now, drink more red wine!